To

Marjorie Switow Fisher

For loving me when I didn't

Believing in me when I couldn't

*Showing me how a woman
can love being a woman*

ACKNOWLEDGMENTS

This book began as a question in late 2010. I'd revisited news coverage of my 1992 Republican National Convention speech and seen the slender, blonde mother of two preschoolers talking to the world. I'd reread the memoir that followed, *My Name is Mary* (Scribner, 1996). I felt as though I knew the woman in that book: She and I were like distant relatives—she was a cousin on my mother's side, perhaps. But we were not the same person. "Who have I become?" I wondered, and this book was born.

Both my book and I are deeply indebted to Dr. Brian Weiss, a philosopher, psychiatrist, and author of uncanny brilliance. It was Brian who first introduced me to the reality of messages given to us and intended for others. He has been a healer in my life, as have Drs. Stuart Seale, Cap Lesesne, Craig Bunnell, and Stephanie Bernik. For most of the past twenty years, I've been diagnosed, treated, and loved by Drs. Melanie Bone in Florida and Steve Grinspoon in Boston, and by the incomparable Dr. Michael Saag in Birmingham, Alabama. Collectively, they've carried me through some very grim hours, and I am grateful.

Many friends and colleagues have joined me in dinner discussions, late-night conversations, e-mail exchanges, phone confabs, moments of hilarity, and hours of hard thought. This book would not be what it is, because I would not be who I am, were it not for Joy Anderson, Stacey Beck, Elisabetta Dami, Dr. Mark Dybul, Kathleen Glynn, Michael Iskowitz, Larry Kramer, Joy Prouty, Judy Sherman, and Stuart White. Suzie Schomaker stands out from any crowd because of her music, but even more because of her soul; she too has shaped this book.

Francine LeFrak has joined me in recent years in service to the East African group known as "the ABATAKA women." When we started out, with the help of Penny Morgan, we intended to teach these women to make jewelry that we could sell on their behalf. That happened. But so did this: On the pretense of teaching, we were learning. The gifted and courageous ABATAKA women brought more wisdom, compassion, and laughter to our work than we could ever have imagined. I'm humbled by these women of Zambia and Rwanda, and by all of Africa's HIV-infected women who hugged me into their communities. With Francine, I am honored to be their partner.

When I paid attention to the book instead of my business, rescue came in the form of marketing guru Lynette Jennings, attorney Jacqueline Miller, accountant Diana Cronin, and advisor Scott Mahoney. Jennifer Reddington and Penny Morgan managed unpredictable twists and turns of clients, sales, and life so I could work on my art and on this book.

Holly Bimba and Patrick Fallon have been the two most critical parts of my "art team" for nearly two decades now, and Dillon Whitlock has helped with every project (planned and unplanned) for just as long. Greg DeWitt joined us a year ago, and Louis Carney has assisted us for years. Without them, I would imagine art more than produce it.

Patrick Schweiss heads the gifted and good people who, together, lead the Sedona International Film Festival; I am their understudy, drawing on their passion and generosity when my own would flag. The Sedona community holds friends and colleagues too numerous to name. Even Elmo—and Kevin, on whose farm Elmo rides—knows that the people of Sedona have no peers. They are, all of them, sources of inspiration, humor and hope.

This book is dedicated to my mother, as was my first memoir. I hope she enjoys this one more. Other family members have shown keen interest in my changing directions, especially as we worked together at the Max M. and Marjorie S. Fisher Foundation: I'm grateful for the special contributions of my siblings Margie, Julie, Phillip, and Jane, and for the leadership with which Douglas Bitonti Stewart has graced us all.

No two people have had a greater impact on this book than my youngest son, Zachary, and his older brother, Max. By the time this book finds distribution, Max will have married Susan Borke and I, very happily, will have witnessed their vows.

The woman in my first memoir, that Mary, was getting ready to die. She wrote her memoir in part as a last will and testament. I remember her. Over the past two decades she has been eclipsed by a Mary who looks at Max and Susan and says, with the joy of a Jewish mother, "So, when are you going to make me a grandmother?"

CONTENTS

Prologue:
Waking Up to Pain

I surfaced, coming up from somewhere deep like a cave or a well or a red-rock canyon. There were lights; even with my eyes closed, I felt them. I heard metal on metal, then voices. Someone walked nearby in squeaky shoes.

I had not yet opened my eyes when I tried to adjust my legs. I moved, barely—but enough to set off fireworks in my chest. I'd known pain before, but this was something of another magnitude, a different species. Pure, stunning, undiluted agony gripped me, sank barbed claws into my flesh, and ripped at me. This was *you-have-no-control* pain, *don't-move* pain, *don't-breathe* pain, *you-can't-even-think* pain. Maybe prayer would help, or maybe profanity, but even speech was unthinkable. It required movement. And movement meant excruciating, staggering torture.

I was still coming to grips with this pain when a voice asked about morphine. I was conscious enough to know that I wanted to scream, "*Yes!*" But moving or speaking was not an option. I tried breathing instead: gentle, shallow breaths. *Breathe.* A different voice said, "It's in the tube . . . It'll work in a minute." *Breathe.*

What was this new agony? Surely it wasn't AIDS. That was a long-ago nightmare—it had been July 1991 when they said I had AIDS. The thing about AIDS is that it doesn't rip your chest out and leave hooks tugging at your bloody muscle. It wastes you. It takes away your immunity so you suffer more slowly, gradually stumbling from colds to pneumonia, from scabs to cancer. It drains you and makes you hate your body. It will even kill you. But it doesn't do what was happening to me now.

No, this wasn't AIDS. This was something else. I knew this was something else.

And I was right. This was January 2012, and I was emerging from surgery. I was back in the System, a body on a gurney, a patient defined by numbers on a clipboard. I was a dot on the nurse's chart, an X over some hours on a calendar page hung outside Operating Room Two. And yet I was a special case. Everyone would be careful around my blood. Everyone knew that this new misery was not my first terminal disease.

I took a gulp of pain and remembered: I was emerging from a mastectomy. I'd never done this before. In six days and a few unimportant hours, I'd gone from *Life is good and getting better* to *You've just had a bilateral mastectomy with node dissection.*

I think it was the brilliant writer and historian Garry Wills who once noted, "The problem with words is, they have meaning." The System knows this, and so it promotes words carefully. When you contract what finally comes to be called "AIDS," they tell you that you have "tested positive for HIV." In 1991, when everyone with that diagnosis was soon leaning on death's door, it seemed better to be HIV-positive than to have AIDS. Healing by rhetoric, I suppose.

Now it seemed somehow important to focus on that word: *mastectomy.* It surely sounded better than surviving an amputation. In fact, the doctors had cut off whatever skin and muscle they could not cut out, leaving me with shards of flesh and pierced by drainage tubes, trying to breathe, waiting for the arrival of my new best friend, morphine. By any reasonable definition, this was an *amputation.*

Either way, it all came back to that little word slipped into the report sent to me, at my request, a mere six days back—and even as a harmless word, it's hard to take: *cancer.*

1

A Letter to My Children

—— SOUL OF SEPARATION ——

When my sons were little, the sweetest moment of the day was when they fell asleep. It brought a joyful quiet, a time divided from the chaos and incessant clatter of the day. No more telephones, no more salesmen, no more noise. Ironically, in being separated from my children by their sleep, in being divided from the noise by the silence—there I was most connected to them and to life. Then came AIDS. In facing separation from all I loved through illness and death, life took on new meaning. I knew again that separation has soul power.

MEMORY OPERATES ON ITS own clock. Four days ago—a mere ninety-six hours—I got teary-eyed over some note I received, and now I can't remember why. But fifty years ago—an entire half century—I hunted for a sweater I wanted to wear that day, and I still remember the cut and color of the sweater, opening the drawer where it was hiding, the dark wood on the dresser. And I recall the weather the day, sixty years ago, that I asked George, my biological father, to explain why he was leaving us. He said, "Ask your mother."

In 1992 I blazed into public awareness like an incoming meteor. I visited most TV screens in America and hijacked a lot of front pages. Two hundred, maybe three hundred million people watched some or all of a thirteen-minute speech I gave. My mother called to read me the story in the *New York Times*. Sixteen years later, when Oxford University Press published *Words of a Century: The Top 100 American Speeches*, 1900–1999, I was in the middle, number 50. That speech resides in my bank of memories just as one of my carefully folded, organized-by-color sweaters rests in my closet. Some people remember it. But it seems odd that those thirteen minutes should define me more than, for example, what Brian said when he left home for the last time as my husband. Our son Max was there. He asked Brian where he was going. Brian said, "Ask your mother."

I'd delivered perhaps a half-dozen speeches in my life before that sweltering night in Houston at the '92 Republican National Convention. I've given maybe a thousand since. Yet I remember more detail from my mostly private speech to the women stored on Rikers Island, delivered a year after Houston, than from the one I gave to the convention crowd.

And then there was Birmingham, Alabama: I was guest preacher for the thirtieth-anniversary memorial of the bombing of the Sixteenth Street Baptist Church, where four Sunday school girls in white dresses were giggling when the bomb tore through the building and their bodies. I remember the hugs after my sermon and the mother who held me tight to whisper, so no one would know, "My son has AIDS." I remember the father who had lifted his daughter's lifeless body from the rubble and, thirty years later, looked up at me as I spoke, quiet tears staining his ebony cheeks. In my memory, I'm a long way from Houston; Birmingham was a moment ago.

Memory and time play tricks. Like looking through a curved glass, some things become exaggerated and others shrink. What were once

Big Moments get reduced to "Oh, I think I remember that." I'm crystal clear about the moment in the fall of 1990 that my friend Joy Anderson changed my life forever by introducing me to the work of psychiatrist Brian Weiss. Ask her about it, though, and she says, wide-eyed, "I did?"

Memories not only speak to me; they are me. They change my decision making, shape my humor, populate my nightmares, and give substance to my art. In some strange but powerful sense, my memory *is* me. To lack certain memories—as those people who suffer amnesia or dementia do—would be to forget, even misplace myself.

Some memories are shared, like the night my father—friend and adviser to then president Richard Nixon—came home from a long day at the White House to find his kitchen full of my friends. We were baking brownies, and he was hungry. He loaded a plate and headed upstairs, and the silence that had descended with his entrance exploded in relieved laughter as my boyfriend of the moment whispered, "The straightest man in America just left President Nixon's Oval Office to fly home and go to bed eating a fistful of marijuana brownies." I've heard that story retold at every high school reunion I've ever attended.

Once I believed that what was done in public carried greater weight, and probably had greater value, than whatever happened out of public sight. I'm not sure—not anymore, now that I am in my mid-sixties—that the public memories matter more or less than the quiet, private ones. It's the mix, the peculiar combination of memories shared and unshared, that make us *us*. And it is the "us" that is important—we individuals who try to unscramble our memories into a clear-eyed and maybe even coherent story of our lives.

I WAS BORN LIZBETH Davis Frehling in Louisville's most beautiful season: spring. It was 1948. My mother had been a wartime bride. Her husband, George Frehling, insisted that their first child, a daughter, be named Lizbeth. Mother never liked the name and, ten weeks later, she arranged a temple ceremony to change it to Mary. The name Frehling became expendable when George left in 1952, and I changed my name once more, after Mother married Max Fisher, an industrialist widower becoming known in Detroit as a philanthropist, who happily adopted my little brother, Phillip, and me.

Our Kentucky years were rich in family. Uncles, aunts, cousins, and grandparents would gather on weekend evenings. Mother sang and Papaharry Switow played the piano, reenacting vaudeville acts and telling dirty stories until my grandmother, Flohoney, roared out of the kitchen, shouting, "Not in front of the children, Harry!"

Detroit was quieter, with more earthly comforts and fewer noisy relatives. After a few years, we acquired staff to manage the kitchen and drivers who took us to school, while Mother became the organizer of Max's social calendar. By the time I began high school, our home had become the gathering place for political power brokers visiting Dad and the site of spectacular dinner parties staged by Mother. Two sisters, Margie and Julie, had been born. Max's daughter from his first marriage, Jane, had left for boarding school, then college, then marriage.

Kingswood was the girls' school half of Kingswood Cranbrook, a storied suburban institution I attended with children of Detroit's other recognized families. During my grade-school years I had already become an organizer, a pleaser, and a caretaker. I organized my sock drawer, kept meticulous notes in my diary, and remembered every necessary detail for my seventh-grade dance. I had a knack for knowing what would make you happy, whether "you" were parent, teacher, friend, or foe, and I'd do whatever it took to please you. As a little girl, I had acted as comforter for my mother in the days after George had left, and eventually I perfected the caregiving role for a series of friends, bosses, lovers, and relatives. Before I left high school I'd become Phillip's protector, Mother's defender, and my class president all four years.

To please my parents, I eventually agreed to follow Jane to college. The University of Michigan was nearby. When asked, I've always said I was there for a semester, but that's not true. After trying it for a few weeks, I began pulling out, one class at a time. I missed Kingswood and the weaving room where I had hidden every time I was sad. I longed for Kingswood's looms—the comforting *clackety-clack* of the looms, the smell of the oiled wood, the feel of the wool. By winter holidays I was back home, visiting Kingswood to weave and looking for work.

I was a philanthropist's daughter who was an organizer, a pleaser, and a caretaker—read: the perfect candidate to help launch a local public television auction. I was soon busy bringing *Sesame Street* to the children of Detroit. Three years later I moved to the local ABC-owned-and-operated station, WXYZ, as producer of its morning show. My ability to organize, desire to please, and willingness to care for others were perfect—*and* I had the invitation lists to my mother's parties and the phone numbers of every candidate and business associate who wanted access to my father. *We need a name to interview? No problem.*

I first worked for free and later was paid a pittance at WXYZ because, my boss said plainly, "You don't need the money." True, I didn't need cash for gas money, rent, and the like; for a sense of self-worth, however, it could've come in handy. People were calling me a "socialite." I heard that word as "freeloader."

Hoping a relationship would make me happy, I married; it didn't last. Thinking I'd find true happiness buried within my Jewish tradition, I moved to Israel; that didn't last either. My self-image, my sense of value, was zero. As I once remembered it, "When I looked at my mother, I saw beauty. When I looked in the mirror, I saw short and fat . . . At any moment I can hear the voices—countless voices over the years—of people looking at me, then saying to one another, 'Isn't it a shame? Such a pretty face. . . .'"

9

RICHARD NIXON CLIMBED THE helicopter steps, waved, and went home to California in disgrace, leaving the White House occupied by Michigan's own Gerald R. Ford, the thirty-eighth president of the United States. After I helped my father organize a successful visit by President Ford to Detroit, the president named me the nation's first female "advance man" on the White House staff. I was honored, and I collected two years of illustrious memories, half the pay of newly hired men, and a great weariness from being the first woman advance man. Being "the first woman who . . ." has its drawbacks.

My mother had learned to cope with her problems by having a drink, and one drink led to another . . . and another. In a moment of blessed desperation around Thanksgiving 1984, she admitted the need for help, Betty Ford personally intervened, and I was quickly organizing her admission and the family's trip to the Betty Ford Center. I went with my mother because I knew she needed me. When she became sober, however, things changed. She no longer needed me to be her caregiver, to shelter her, or to show my love by pretending that she was not an alcoholic. She could very competently organize her own life, thank you very much.

Meanwhile, the center staff had observed my patterns of obsession, some drinking, and plenty of self-loathing. I denied that I had a problem with drinking and pointed to how well I was holding my life together. "You know, dear," said Mrs. Ford kindly, "you don't need to wait for the elevator to get to the basement before you get off." Mother was soon back home, sober, and now I was a resident of the Betty Ford Center.

I moved from the center to Parkside Lodge in the mountains of Colorado. In these two places I experienced, for the first time, an authentic spirituality together with the revelation that I was an artist. If there is a dividing line in my life, it isn't the bombshell of my HIV diagnosis or thirteen minutes in Houston; it is this time of quiet discovery.

My Jewishness had been cultural but not particularly spiritual, and Israel had not been a long experience for me. Piety was not part of my lifestyle. When at the Center I lost my roles as pleaser and caretaker, it was as if my purpose for existence evaporated. If I was no longer the adult child who took care of everything, if that was no longer my job, then what? In surrendering to the reality that I was not my role—that what I did was not who I am—I found peace. It was not a white-light experience. It arrived over a period of weeks, first at the Center and then at the Lodge. But it happened. I experienced it. It was real, tangible, undeniable. By spring of '85 I was filling pages of my journal with poetry and prayers acknowledging that my "endless emptiness" had been "filled by God."

Looking back, I now imagine this new awareness prepared me for the simultaneous discovery that art was an inextricable part of who I am. I'd seen creativity at work throughout my childhood. Mother designed blouses while living in Louisville. Papaharry, who owned a string of theaters, had a drawing board where I spent hours watching him sketch, draw, and color—turning theater concepts into near-architectural renderings. But it was at Parkside that, for the first time, I began to understand what it meant to express what is in one's soul by speaking through one's hands. I began to draw, and once I started, I could not stop.

I left Parkside Lodge sober and grounded, certain that life had a purpose beyond organizing my sock drawers and family trips, and I headed for New York to pursue art. I took lessons. I studied colors and textures, styles and trends, the power of light and the use of darkness. I experimented. Brian Campbell, a seasoned artist and designer, became my mentor long before he became my husband. As we sat together one night, he pulled from his wallet a crumpled piece of paper on which he'd written a quote from sculptor David Smith: "Art is made from dreams and visions, and things not known, and least of all from things that can be said. It comes from the inside of who you are, when you face yourself." I understood.

A sense of the Divine has been with me ever since I left the Betty Ford Center. And since Parkside, my passion has been not organizing, pleasing, or caregiving (except when this is defined as "being a mother"), but art. It was Brian who nurtured me through the tender years of emergence when I would fall back into uncertainty, who taught me in his own way that I mattered, who encouraged me to explore things not known, with a quiet "It's okay, Mar; it's okay. Try again. . . ."

11

I HEARD MY SON'S heartbeat for the first time on my birthday, April 6, 1987. Brian and I had married the previous January, and I was pregnant a month after we got home from the honeymoon. My journals remind me what I might have otherwise forgotten: I felt the baby kicking, "like bubbles inside" (May 30). Brian cupped my tummy while our Max delivered a clean kick (June 16). I was able to know my own joy, to write that I had "never been happier, or felt better, in my entire life."

Brian and I moved from New York City to Florida to be closer to my family as we raised our own. While I prepared for Max's arrival, Mother and Brian were planning the opening of the Harrison Gallery, named after Papaharry. When Max arrived, my attention shifted almost entirely to him—and to an ugly postpartum infection that required surgery. By the time I was healing, Brian and mother were largely busy or gone, buying art for the gallery. Told I'd be unable to sustain another pregnancy, I began organizing an adoption. Shortly after Max turned two, in the fall of '89, Zachary became our second son.

Motherhood was even better than I could have imagined. Marriage was worse. My weight gains during pregnancy and my health issues had frozen Brian's interest in intimacy. I assumed he'd perk up when life got back to normal. But normal didn't happen. Brian moved out, and the divorce, an ugly affair, was final in August 1990. I grieved our marriage but stayed sober. I was ecstatic about being a mother, and people were buying my art.

I read *Many Lives, Many Masters*, Brian Weiss's first book, at my friend Joy's suggestion. With uncommon grace and humility, this brilliant man blended psychiatry with spirituality. He had an active practice in Miami, and by the summer of 1991 I was driving from my home nearby to see him weekly. He led me through meditations and reflections, offered therapeutic insights, and urged me to stay open to what was to come because, he would say, something "very big, very important" was on the horizon, just out of sight.

I didn't feel very big or important. My art was improving, though I was not yet on a level to intimidate Picasso or Van Gogh. But with Brian Weiss's guidance, I felt spiritually grounded, open to being led, and grateful—for my art and, especially, my children. I did not know then where all this would lead, but even then, I knew it mattered.

What I now know is that saying "it mattered" is feeble. In fact, it changed my life.

I KNEW WHEN I married Brian Campbell that he'd given up drugs as I'd given up alcohol; I knew he inspired the artist within me; and I knew he loved me. What more was there to know, really?

Well, there's this: He called me on Wednesday, July 3, 1991, to say he'd just received the test results and he was HIV-positive. He was hysterical over the phone, disoriented, fading in and out. I heard him say "suicide" and told him I was coming to see him. I found him at his apartment pacing the floor, shoving his hands through his thinning hair, crying, "What will I do?" At his next words, I stopped breathing.

"What about Max?"

I stayed with Brian until he calmed down and promised he wouldn't hurt himself. Then I got into my car and wondered if I should drive or vomit.

It was a holiday weekend, and I couldn't get tested until the following week. So Monday, July 8, was the day. Beginning July 9, I called the clinic every day to ask for my results, and every day I was told they weren't yet available. Days and nights crawled by. Two weeks after Brian's call to me, the antiseptic, disembodied voice of the nurse at the clinic came down the phone line: "Just a moment, the doctor wants to speak to you."

The next voice was of a man, a stranger, saying, "I'm sorry, Mary, your test is positive."

I'd had days to prepare myself to hear those words, but I wasn't prepared. What I did know—what I'd thought about incessantly—was that Zachary had probably been spared by adoption, but since I was positive, Max had been exposed.

I'd called the clinic at the last moment before boarding a plane with my brother to meet our parents in Europe for a long-promised vacation. I barely stayed composed enough to kiss Max and Zack goodbye. I grabbed at Phillip, sobbing. Jolly as always, and no doubt imagining I simply didn't want to leave the boys, he said soothingly, "It's okay, Mar— we're only going to be gone a week."

13

WE WERE AIRBORNE BEFORE I was able to take stock of the situation. My thoughts were scrambled: *If your father abandons you, your mother might get you another one. If you're an alcoholic, you might try recovery. If you're lonely, you could reach out to others. If you're childless, you could adopt. But if you have AIDS, you die.*

Mother knew the moment she saw me. The tables had turned: In the hours after my biological father had left us, I had crawled into her bed and, in my best four-year-old voice, reassured her, "Don't cry. Me here." If once I had been her comforter, now she was mine.

Telling my father was beyond imagination. I had planned to remain calm, as he would want, and lay out the facts. But just looking at him broke my heart. In tears, I explained that Brian had AIDS and I was infected. "What does that mean?" he asked honestly. He knew as much about AIDS as most Americans did at the time: next to nothing. I tried to evade the question, so he asked again and again: "But what will happen?"

Finally, amid the utter silence, I said it: "I will die, and Max may die too."

I feared my father would have a heart attack, but he stayed calmer than I had expected. He did not fully understand the meaning of HIV—that it led to AIDS, and that AIDS led inevitably to the grave. I realized all this when I heard his familiar question: "Okay, how do we fix it?"

I explained there was no fix, no cure.

"We'll see about that" was his reply.

I flew home to meet Dr. Henry Murray in New York City and have Max tested. "Hank" truly championed my cause—he wasn't going to tolerate the agonizing lag I'd experienced between *my* test and the findings—but the wait was still unbearable. Thirty indescribable hours after testing Max, Hank called. "Max is fine," he said.

I paused. "Say it again, please?"

"Max's test is negative," Hank assured me. "Max is fine. He's okay. Max is negative."

And so the truth was known. I was following Brian down the road to AIDS, but Max and Zachary had been spared. "Thank you," I breathed into the phone so Hank could hear. "Thank you, thank you, thank you."

14

I DIDN'T KNOW WHOM to tell what. Ignorance of the virus was still keen enough to make people fear, say, drinking water from a glass I'd touched. Prejudice about the virus gave AIDS a reputation as a dirty disease contracted through dirty sex or dirty needles by dirty people. I had small children to protect from community vitriol. I was frightened of what would happen if the news slipped out.

President and Mrs. Ford were summering at their home in Beaver Creek, Colorado, when I flew out to tell them. The president took in the news with somber puffs on his pipe, raged for a bit about Brian, then promised he'd do anything he could to help. Betty, on the other hand, had accepted the news with motherly calm. "And now what are you going to do to help women?" she asked.

I had been focused on myself and my family, wondering how we would cope. Mrs. Ford offered the beginnings of a new perspective, suggesting I refocus on a more valuable approach: serving others. When, some weeks later, I asked if she thought I should go public, she was slow to answer. Eventually she said, "Yes." But her "yes" seemed to carry memories, perhaps of her own experience going public about her breast cancer and her alcoholism. After a moment, she said emphatically, "Once you say it in public, Mary, you can never take it back. It's in public, attached to you, forever."

My parents and siblings were ambivalent about my decision to go public. Owing to real threats, Dad had needed armed protection for years. We'd watched others wander into the vulnerability of the public spotlight. Betty Ford had spoken the hard truth: Once you're in the public eye, you can't escape it again. Readers can be mean. Viewers can turn brutal. Reporters can tell your story or slant it. Letter writers can violate your sense of safety and decency. My family's hesitation was based on the security of privacy and the desire for protection.

If I leaned on friends and family during the closing months of 1991, I leaned even harder on Brian Weiss. He kept pointing to what he called "the bigger picture," and together we sought guidance. Week by week, listening to Brian's calming voice, I looked for some purpose in my dying. But I couldn't find it, couldn't see it. I was briefly inspired by Magic Johnson's upbeat November 1991 press conference announcing that he was HIV-positive. I wondered how he had done that, how he had faced the public with a smile on his face.

In New Mexico a month after my diagnosis, I met Sally Fisher, a longtime figure in New York and Los Angeles theater and, by the time I met her, a force in the American AIDS community. I told her my story, and she told me about life on the road to AIDS. What I remembered most after she left was her closing remark: "I need to tell you that we've been waiting for someone like you to come along. You're not a gay man. You're not a Santa Fe liberal. You're in the All-American Republican Power Family: sweet blonde mom with two cute kids. You're just what we've needed."

I didn't feel needed. I felt angry, foolish, anxious, deceived, and sorry for myself.

God *will finish* what I cannot complete.

I MOPED INTO 1992 an unknown mother and struggling artist. That I'd been left with a nasty virus was a private matter. Only a few dozen relatives, doctors, and friends knew. Then came the calls letting me know the news had somehow leaked and some media inquiries were floating around.

So in January, I talked to two national journalists I knew and trusted: Ann Compton and Diane Sawyer. Both echoed Betty Ford's warning that "once public, always public," and both offered to help. I decided I'd simultaneously offer my story to Diane, who made it a segment on ABC's *Primetime Live*, and to my hometown *Detroit Free Press*, whose editor, Joe Stroud, had a reputation for unflinching honesty. Joe offered up Frank Bruni, now a columnist with the *New York Times*, from his stable of gifted young writers. Frank flew to Florida to interview me and stayed four days. On Thursday, February 13, 1992, my story was told on the opening three pages of the *Free Press*, and a week later it was shown on Diane's national feature.

So I was public. The story was picked up in all the predictable places, including South Florida, where I lived. Suddenly I couldn't shop for a cabbage without being recognized, and the recognition wasn't comfortable. Our home became a jangle of phone calls, a crowd of journalists, photographers, and friends. I did my best to shelter Zack and Max, but chaos and noise dominated.

Then, two days after Diane's special, everything stopped. Quiet descended. I was, literally, yesterday's news. So that had been that.

Frank Bruni's story had quoted me as saying, "I want to help people get rid of the fear," and, "It doesn't matter how you got it. It can happen to anyone." Those two messages were really all I had in my arsenal. I'd said what I had to say. It seemed to me that my moment in the spotlight was over.

IN THE WEEKS FOLLOWING the media flurry, I sank into the routine of preparing to become ill and die. I wrote long, long entries in Max's and Zack's journals so they'd know me when they were older and I was gone. I was never tempted by suicide during this time, but these were hard, painful days. I tried to be happy around the boys, but nights were grim. Once the sun set, it became hard to deny my "reality": Life wasn't fair. I didn't deserve this. At times I knew I was just feeling sorry for myself, but that didn't stop me.

Meanwhile, Brian Weiss was still talking about "big and important messages." It seemed to me that he must have had something and some-one else in mind: I'd told my story, delivered my two messages, and suc-ceeded mostly in getting strangers to point me out to their children. I'd become an object lesson of some kind.

I was surprised to find that my star hadn't quite fizzled when the American Foundation for AIDS Research (amfAR) invited me to accept an honor from Elizabeth Taylor at a fund-raising dinner in New York City on April 13. It would be a glittering affair, naturally, full of celebrity and diamonds. I'd be asked to accept the award and then "say a few words." I figured I could walk to the podium to receive a plaque of some kind. "Saying a few words" seemed a bit more daunting.

I'd been trying to organize an event in Michigan with Magic Johnson, who'd been a star in high school and college there. The event wasn't com-ing together, but in the course of trying, I met a consultant and writer who began helping me put words to my feelings: A. James Heynen. I asked for Jim's help with the amfAR event, and when he sent some notes and a few paragraphs, I took them to Brian Weiss, who was enthusiastic. "Say that," Brian said with delight. "Say it exactly that way." I did, and to my amazement, it worked.

Since my message was my story, telling my story seemed like the obvious thing to do. But it took both practice and courage to tell it in public. A month after the amfAR event, I was to speak at a luncheon for another New York charity and this time I read aloud a letter written to my children. The response was instantaneous. Publishers, charities, and AIDS organizations wanted to reprint it. Even more meaningful to me, other HIV-infected mothers who read it in magazines wanted a copy. The letter's closing became the title for my first book:

Tonight when I tucked each of you into bed, I said to you what you've heard me say every night of your lives. Since the moment you came from my body, Max, and the hour you were placed in my arms, Zachary, I have known that I would, one day, have to give you up.

17

And so, each night, I rehearse for the day when I must give you over. That is why, as I reach for the day's last kiss and hug, you always hear me say the same four words: "Sleep with the angels."

Love, Mom

REGARDLESS OF THE SUPPORT I was receiving from family, friends, even strangers, this disease had drawn a line between me and the society to which I had always belonged. Intellectually, I knew about stigma, judgmentalism, prejudice. But I had never before been the object of it. AIDS in America was (and still is) an illness that belongs to "them," not "us." I was being transformed into one of "them." And I didn't like it.

Now, two decades later, I realize how powerful it was, this shared community attitude toward AIDS. I felt as though I had been evicted from my own life, my culture. I was on the outside looking in. I had embarrassed my family. I felt ashamed.

During my time at the Betty Ford Center, I'd first read the line from Bill Wilson, founder of AA: "Pain is the touchstone of all spiritual progress." Pain may be a touchstone—something that tests our mettle—but I didn't sense much spiritual progress in the silence and sorrow of those days. I was hanging on, still sober, but sad.

When I was struck with a second diagnosis twenty years later, this time with cancer, I saw with perfect clarity the stark contrast with what I had experienced in 1992. Among the smorgasbord of feelings that rolled in with the cancer, there was not a shred of shame. Friends, family, loved ones, neighbors—people came rushing in to comfort and encourage me, and I let them. They rallied to my support, rooted for my surgeons, prayed for my healing. Never once did I experience the terror of being excluded, the shame of being judged, as I did after my diagnosis with HIV.

I still have remnants of that AIDS-inspired fear and shame. I can recite all the reasons it doesn't make sense. I can write books and give speeches explaining why others ought never to feel it. But cancer taught me the truth: We've infused American AIDS with so much shame that women and men at risk are too afraid to be tested; they'd rather die than know. And once you *are* diagnosed positive, you head for silence, not support.

If you have cancer in America, you look for a great doctor. If you have AIDS, you look for a place to hide.

2

Walking Into Evil

──────── EVERY SOUL ────────

Remembering her, I realize that every soul tells its own story. She had promised me that, once on the medications, she'd never stop. But her husband said she was shameful; he left. His family took the children. She felt her neighbors' accusing eyes, judging her guilty for a virus she never understood. Now, preparing to bury her, I heard her soul's story of piercing hopelessness. And I remembered again that every soul speaks, rarely using words.

─────────────────────────────

THE CROWD THAT GATHERED in South Florida on March 21, 1996, was innocent. They probably did not deserve the angry speech I gave them. They were, for the most part, kind donors and gifted staff involved with regional community foundations. But their speaker that day—me— was motivated to make a point, and that point bordered on accusation.

It was nearly five years past my diagnosis and four years since the convention speech. What had started with Betty Ford's question about helping others and continued with a personal letter to my children had swelled into speeches, articles, testimony, and other forms of activism. I had relocated from Florida to the outskirts of Washington, DC, nearly three years earlier, and this was among my first return engagements in the community where I had chosen to go public. I was less than three minutes into my address when I admitted that what had frozen me in a state of indecision for months after my diagnosis was my fear of rejection by my community. This would hardly have been an offensive sentiment— except that this particular audience, of course, had been my community at the time.

I might as well have said, "I was scared witless about how you would treat us." I spruced it up a little, but not too much: "I dreaded both my own and my family's risk of being judged and condemned and eventually ostracized," I explained. "What the virus itself cannot kill—the human spirit, one's sense of dignity and hope—is precisely what our judgmental- ism and our indifference attack. Given free rein, it does its own killing."

AIDS is not good for your self-image. Practically everyone with this disease contracts a version of the "leprosy complex"—the feeling that he or she should walk down the sidewalk preceded by a warning for oth- ers, crying out, "Unclean! Unclean!" It was helpful knowing that others with AIDS felt the same way. But this didn't *get rid of* the complex or the fear in which it was rooted. I had felt uncertain about myself in the past, maybe even unworthy, and AIDS called those feelings back to the fore.

About a year after my diagnosis with HIV, I was in New York City and a friend asked that I go up to Harlem to meet a dozen extraordinary young women enrolled in a program named Stand Up Harlem. Most were in their early twenties, some pregnant, all HIV-positive. Almost casually we fell into a discussion of what we'd change about our lives if we could. We laughed as we discussed (as women do) men we could have avoided. We got back on topic when LaShane spoke of wanting to feel better because "it's hard to be patient with the kids when you're sick." Chondra said, "A cure would be nice," and several of us said we needed to find someone we could really trust to care for our children when we were gone.

What I could not have known at the time was how clearly I would remember Chrystine, a beautiful teenager who softly spoke her truth: "I'd really like to have cancer." We waited through her pause. "If I had cancer, I could tell the truth and people wouldn't hate me. My family wouldn't be so ashamed of me. I could go home. They'd let me in. If I had cancer, they'd love me again."

I've tried them both now, AIDS and cancer. Chrystine had it right. Each disease brings the physical reality of suffering and a dread of what lies ahead. But only one of these unwanted gifts comes wrapped in shame.

IF IT HADN'T BEEN for the Democrats, I'd never have spoken to all those Republicans.

In May 1992 I visited Washington, DC, to ask Republican members of Congress to support AIDS research and develop compassionate policies toward HIV patients and families. The senator who was organizing platform hearings for the upcoming Republican National Convention to be held in Houston invited me to "give testimony." It sounded like a good idea. I said yes, and later that month I was at a witness table in Salt Lake City, urging Republicans to "lift our shroud of silence, speak boldly in a voice of compassion, and do justice to the tradition which brought us all here today." My appearance garnered enough media attention that, when the Democrats announced that Elizabeth Glaser and Bob Hattoy would address their New York City convention in July, journalists naturally wondered, "What about the Republicans—will they have someone speak on AIDS too?"

In July I spoke at the International Conference on AIDS in Amsterdam, which got me some more media coverage back home. The *Houston Chronicle* ran a July 21 story pushing convention planners to say yes or no on addressing the issue of AIDS. I didn't know it then, but the *Washington Post* and the *New York Times* had been pestering convention leaders daily with the same question, sometimes with my name attached. Then *USA Today* ran a long feature by national correspondent

Patricia Edmonds discussing my story, my father's Republican credentials, and AIDS in the streets and at the conventions. Within hours of this article's appearance, Patty Presock, the brilliant administrative aide to President George H. W. Bush, contacted me. "It's in the works," she said.

In the United States, a national convention historically lasts four days. Most of the real work is done away from the limelight of each evening's prime-time televised coverage. Convention speakers are generally allotted two minutes (for an introduction), three minutes (for commentary), or five minutes (for remarks). Perhaps two dozen heavyweights, including the presidential and the vice presidential nominees, get more than five minutes. Because the Democrats had put Elizabeth and Bob on prime time, because the story had played prominently in the media, perhaps because I was a novelty, and certainly because President Bush gave a nod to the idea—I won what was described as a five-minute speaking part for the evening of Wednesday, August 19.

The convention organizers were taking a risk by putting AIDS on their agenda. AIDS protestors were three-deep outside the White House every day, and anger was sky-high among the dying and those who loved them. Gay publications were bashing the president, the administration, and anyone and anything that wore the title "Republican." At the convention itself, when President Bush's car was identified, protestors began pelting it with liquid-filled condoms. Some of them were able to rally just enough strength from their AIDS-ravaged bodies to make the pitch. The noise of protest was everywhere political leaders gathered. Fury bordered dangerously close to riot. From a Republican leadership perspective, there was no such thing as "a good AIDS story."

Convention planners were set to host a four-day gathering of powerful Republican leaders with the world's media on hand. They recognized that, in the eyes of protestors, this was an unparalleled opportunity to showcase their protests, their anger, and their dying. The decision whether to invite me was a risk-management assessment: Elizabeth had basically told the nation that President Bush had killed her child. Republican organizers had to book a speaker in hopes it would appear the parties were balanced on this issue; either that, or they could let the issue stay out on the streets, keep it off their agenda, and treat AIDS as a disease of Democrats. My story and pedigree made it difficult to deny that Republicans were just as susceptible, but even that did not mean the issue would go on Houston's agenda.

The moment my appearance was announced, a torrent of advice poured in. I was lobbied in person and at second hand, through acquaintances and siblings and strangers. The most aggressive pressure came from those with a financial stake—people in the AIDS industry—who wanted more money for things like drug research or clinic construction. The one place from which I heard very little was the AIDS community itself—the people living with the disease. Sally Fisher and other friends offered support, but I don't recall any of them telling me what to say. Looking back, I imagine they had their own fears. Would I be used as a poster child for Republican political claims? Would I embarrass the cause rather than advance it?

Standing apart from everyone else, in fact and in my memory, was the ever-faithful Brian Weiss. His counsel, offered without a shred of doubt, was consistent. "Speak the truth," he said, "and tell them what you've experienced, because that's how you've received the truth. If you can tell *your* truth, you can make a difference."

The days leading up to the RNC were being filled with people and projects, but it was becoming no clearer to me what specifically I should say in Houston. I liked Brian's point: I should tell *my* truth. But I wasn't sure what my truth was.

SHAME CAN BE EARNED. We can do something so wretched that we feel, rightly, ashamed. But shame can also be an emotional response to something over which we have no control, such as the shame felt by a woman who has been raped or a child who has been abused. Why do we feel ashamed about something we did not condone and could not prevent? The answer isn't clear to me, but listen to the testimony of so many who have survived rape and other abuse, and you'll hear more than you want to know about the irrational power of shame.

Shame can also be taught to us. An African American child can be taught shame about her blackness. A Native American child can be taught to feel ashamed of his history and traditions, his language and the dance of his ancestors. In that literary drama familiar to so many

> If we are to make a **difference** we will—all of us—need to make a *commitment* to break the silence. The **greatest enemy** isn't a virus. It's **silence**.

American students, Hester Prynne wore the scarlet letter *A* because her community *wanted* her to experience shame. And a person with AIDS can be taught that she's dirty or he's undesirable, as if the disease comes not from a virus but from a moral failing.

From long before I knew my own diagnosis, I believed no one should be ashamed of having a virus, but of course it was an abstract belief then—the sort one describes when discussing "what-ifs" at a cocktail party. I would *tut-tut* over right-wing intolerance and crazy attacks on those who suffered and died. But once I had the virus, my belief was no longer an intellectual exercise.

The power of stigma, of community prejudice and personal discrimination, is enormous. Fear and intimidation become effective tools used by someone constructing a campaign to define who is worthy and who is not—or, if you prefer, who is truly human and who is less than human. First we observe that others aren't like "us"—we establish a "we." Then we point out that "they" are different, are not like us. Then *they* comes to mean "less than": That is, *we* are the model of what it means to be human, and *they* are not. *They* are less than human, less than desirable. It makes sense that, for our safety and the safety of our children, *we* should be separated from *them*, segregated. By the time we arrive at this stage, we've paved the road to Auschwitz.

Admittedly, it's a long way from sunny suburban Florida to the gas chambers of Auschwitz or Dachau, but during my first year with the virus I began to see—to experience—how the dots are connected. By virtue of an accident of biological history, the initial outbreak of AIDS in America occurred within the nation's gay communities. When the virus found me, a decade after the disease was labeled "gay cancer," I began to have experiences that might otherwise have been the exclusive province of gay men. By the close of 1992 I would say publicly that some discoveries I'd made since my diagnosis "were painful. I was certain, when I began, that people of good will would respond eagerly to an honest appeal. I was wrong. I'd grossly miscalculated the evil some would visit on this nation's gay communities, if they could."

One incident in particular—such a little thing, really—ate at me. A month or so after I'd gone public, Max told me he was the only child in his class who'd not been allowed to have a stuffed animal "visit overnight" at home. I assumed Max was confused, or perhaps he was being disciplined for some reason. But when I made the usual parental inquiries, I discovered Max had told the truth. Someone had feared that the fuzzy bear or cuddly kitten or whatever it was would come back to school stained with the AIDS virus.

This was not the stuff of which evening newscasts are made. But it signaled something new for me: My children were being impacted by ignorance that attempted to justify stigma. A bit later, I would write:

> *I was not raised in the Jewish ghetto of Warsaw. I'd only heard stories of the camps. No one in Papaharry's tradition had been sold at auction or whipped raw along the edge of a cotton field. This was my first experience in the school of stigma, teaching me firsthand that quiet prejudice grows out of common fear, that whispered ignorance leads to blatant discrimination.*

The fire of maternal anger had been lit, and it would not be extinguished easily; in some very tangible sense, it is unquenchable. I added these thoughts on the matter:

If I'd encountered sex discrimination in both my television and White House experiences, I hadn't understood it clearly enough to fight back effectively. Besides, Mary was a pleaser, not a fighter. But now Mary was a mother. You attack Max or threaten Zachary and, so help me God, I will fight.

For most AIDS advocates, the enemy is the virus. I understand. I support their war. But as it developed, *my* truth had (and still has) as much to do with values as with the virus. *My* truth is that a married Republican woman could contract AIDS in her marriage—and be no more guilty or virtuous than anyone else with the virus. She has no more and no less reason for shame than anyone else does.

Meanwhile, to my relief, almost simultaneous with my first experiences of stigma came moments of unexpected compassion. I had sailed into this period of my life thinking that compassion was a nice emotion, a pleasant character trait. I had no idea what it looked like when given moral muscle. I was beginning to see that power now, to recognize what Viktor Frankl meant when he recalled the Holocaust and wrote: "We who lived in the concentration camps can remember the men who walked through the huts comforting others, giving away their last piece of bread."

I saw such compassion up close when I first encountered AIDS caregivers. In hospices, they would care for those creeping toward death's door. These caregivers would clean the sheets without complaint, touch fevered brows with an angel's grace, and then retreat to the kitchen with others to grieve, and quit, and cry. I could see why. What was incredible was that, within ten minutes, they'd straighten their shoulders, put on their smiles, and go back to their patients again. Even the thought of such compassion is breathtaking. The reality of it—in the camps, among those wasting with AIDS—was death-defying.

MY FATHER HADN'T SEEN the speech until five hours before I was scheduled to deliver it. "Some speech," he said after reading it. "Are you going to be able to say it all?" He feared I'd lose my emotional balance.

By that time, after reflecting on that first year after my diagnosis, I had discovered my truth: Stigma is evil, compassion is divine, and I'd promised my children not a victim but a mother. Here is how I explained it a few months after the convention:

I went public knowing that, sooner or later, [Max and Zachary] would pass judgment on me. They would wonder if I had run from my own fears or faced them; if I had avoided the hard questions or accepted them; if I had merely praised good values or had lived them; if I had struggled to improve their lives or abandoned them. It was not heroism that drew me into the public limelight . . . it was fear. I did not want to fail my children.

But that night in Houston, climbing the steps under the podium, preparing for the phalanx of blinding lights and the din of thousands of voices, people chatting with one another, I felt more than just an aching fear. I felt a rush of terror. The audience I was about to face would either ignore or jeer me. AIDS picketers outside would throw things as we drove out. My heart was pounding and my mind was racing. Then I heard myself think, as clear as day, *God, help me to say it the way they need to hear it.* I was immediately, totally calmed.

A voice said, "Okay, Mary, come on up." It was the stage manager who would station me behind the podium. I couldn't see him.

I asked if he'd put an elevator step behind the podium to compensate for my height.

"Yes" came the voice from the dark.

I climbed out while a video introduction played to a darkened stadium. I steadied myself, placing my hands on the podium. And when the lights came on, I found myself looking into the president's box, where Mr. and Mrs. Ford were seated next to my mother and father. Phillip was there too, looking nervous. I began:

Less than three months ago, at platform hearings in Salt Lake City, I asked the Republican Party to lift the shroud of silence which has been draped over the issue of HIV/AIDS. I have come tonight to bring our silence to an end.

My voice echoed over the chatter that rippled through the crowd. Was anyone listening?

> *I bear a message of challenge, not self-congratulation. I want your attention, not your applause. I would never have asked to be HIV-positive. But I believe that in all things there is a good purpose, and so I stand before you, and before the nation, gladly. . . .*

A few people along the right aisle stopped talking and turned toward me—but not many.

> *In the context of an election year, I ask you—here in this great hall, or listening in the quiet of your home—to recognize that the AIDS virus is not a political creature. It does not care whether you are Democrat or Republican. It does not ask whether you are black or white, male or female, gay or straight, young or old.*

I was getting to my truth. It felt right. I thought the hall was getting quieter.

> *Tonight I represent an AIDS community whose members have been reluctantly drafted from every segment of American society. Though I am white, and a mother, I am one with a black infant struggling with tubes in a Philadelphia hospital. Though I am female, and contracted this disease in marriage, and enjoy the warm support of my family, I am one with the lonely gay man sheltering a flickering candle from the cold winds of his family's rejection.*
>
> *This is not a distant threat; it is a present danger . . . And we have helped it along—we have killed each other—with our ignorance, our prejudice, and our silence.*
>
> *We may take refuge in our stereotypes, but we cannot hide there long. Because HIV asks only one thing of those it attacks: Are you human? And this is the right question: Are you human? Because people with HIV have not entered some alien state of being. They are human. They have not earned cruelty and they do not deserve meanness. They don't benefit from being isolated or treated as outcasts.*

Each of them is exactly what God made: a person. Not evil, deserving of our judgment; not victims, longing for our pity. People. . . .

I glanced down, into the press pit just below, and saw Steven Bradley, a friend. He was grinning. As I spoke, he pulled off his long-sleeved shirt, leaned back, and stuck out his chest, all the while wearing that goofy grin. I could read his T-shirt: Emblazoned in bright red letters was NO ONE HERE KNOWS I'M HIV-POSITIVE! I tried to smile at him and moved toward the final two minutes and ten seconds of copy. Now I was speaking to my fellow pilgrims along the road to AIDS:

You are HIV-positive but dare not say it. You have lost loved ones, but you dared not whisper the word AIDS. *You weep silently; you grieve alone.*

I have a message for you: It is not you who should feel shame; it is we. We who tolerate ignorance and practice prejudice, we who have taught you to fear. We must lift our shroud of silence, making it safe for you to reach out for compassion . . .

Someday our children will be grown. My son Max, now four, will take the measure of his mother; my son Zachary, now two, will sort through his memories. I may not be here to hear their judgments, but I know already what I hope they are.

I want my children to know that their mother was not a victim. She was a messenger. I do not want them to think, as I once did, that courage is the absence of fear; I want them to know that courage is the strength to act wisely when most we are afraid. I want them to have the courage to step forward when called by their nation, or their party, and give leadership—no matter what the personal cost. I ask no more of you than I ask of myself or of my children.

To the millions of you who are grieving, who are frightened, who have suffered the ravages of AIDS firsthand: Have courage, and you will find support.

To the millions who are strong, I issue this plea: Set aside prejudice and politics to make room for compassion and sound policy.

To my children, I make this pledge: I will not give in, Zachary, because I draw my courage from you. Your silly giggle gives me hope.

Your gentle prayers give me strength. And you, my child, give me reason to say to America, "You are at risk." And I will not rest, Max, until I have done all I can to make your world safe. I will seek a place where intimacy is not the prelude to suffering.

I will not hurry to leave you, my children. But when I go, I pray that you will not suffer shame on my account.

To all within the sound of my voice, I appeal: Learn with me the lessons of history and of grace, so my children will not be afraid to say the word AIDS when I am gone. Then their children, and yours, may not need to whisper it at all.

God bless the children, and bless us all. Good night.

It was over. There was a moment of silence and then a roar, thousands of flashbulbs, and a voice nearby, saying, "God bless you." It was over.

THE HOURS AND DAYS immediately following the speech were mostly consumed in media interviews and, when I was not in the public eye, with my children. By the weekend, news reports were fading into editorial analyses. The *Miami Herald* amused us with a headline about my speech: GRACE AMID GRINCHES. Brent Staples told readers of the *New York Times* that I'd been alone in TEACHING MERCY TO REPUBLICANS.

The day after my convention speech, my father had a breakfast meeting. He came back to the hotel and said, "Mary, you've changed my life."

My heart sank. Had he suffered some vicious comment about his daughter with AIDS?

He went on, "When they introduced me this morning, the host said, 'Ladies and gentlemen, it gives me pleasure to present Mary Fisher's father.'" He smiled and added, "They gave me a standing ovation."

TWENTY YEARS PAST HOUSTON, I am still sometimes introduced as "the lady who gave that speech." Fewer and fewer people remember it, of course, as fewer and fewer people remember the electric tension then surrounding AIDS in America. For some, I'm not instantly recognizable. My children have grown into adulthood, antiretroviral drugs have kept me alive, and my hair is shorter now, easier to take care of.

My ability to sense prejudice has grown keener, and my patience with it has shrunk. My truth, however, has remained largely unchanged. You may say, if you wish, that I am a "victim" of cancer—although I still have a visceral dislike for the word—because I know you mean only that I'm dealing with the disease. But if you call me an "AIDS victim," I'm likely to transport myself instantly back to that warm March day in South Florida, when kindly philanthropists gathered for lunch and got a bellyful of me.

Somewhere between their salads and forgettable desserts, they heard me remark:

> *Babies and surgical patients are said to be infected through no fault of their own. They are the "innocent victims." By implication, all others chose to have the illness and "got what they had coming to them." By this line of thinking, hemophiliacs should be pitied and babies with AIDS should be cuddled by First Ladies. But all others are guilty. People with AIDS are not merely infected; they are corrupted.*

33

Shame and stigma—two sides of a single coin—became the object of my message to the world, *my* truth. I took up that coin early and have not yet put it down. Nor do I intend to. If occasionally I speak too quickly, pass my own judgment about judgmentalism too easily, then I do my best to make amends. I'm learning to live with my anger, including the anger at being infected with AIDS. But I have no intention of learning to tolerate shame.

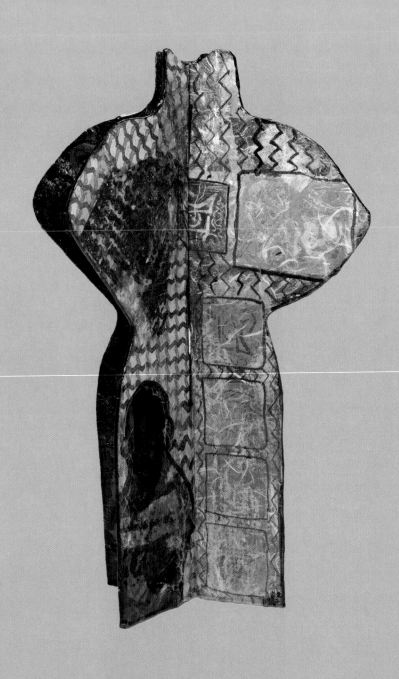

3

If I Die Before I Wake

———————— PENSIVE SOUL ————————

Worst is the middle of the night. I'm almost
awake—ghosts of death crawl under the
sheets with me. It's 1995 again, everywhere I
turn, new friends wasting into skeletons. It's
1993, Brian, once my laughing husband, is
holding my hand as his fingers turn blue and
cold. It's 2006, African children are unable to
laugh, to breathe, to nurse. I've loved them all
and saved not one of them. Not one. Not one.
Then come early light and coffee. My soul has
been shaken again. It is quiet, pensive.

THE AMERICAN VIEW OF death is, in a word, *denial.* Expressed as a contraction, our response to dying is "Don't."

The young know it can't happen to them, despite statistics on urban manslaughter. Newlyweds think of children, not caskets. We love sharing photographs of newborns; we'd rather not see Grandma in her coffin. In our relative youth, we seek out an infinite variety of improbable appetite suppressants and sexual stimulants. As we age toward fifty or sixty, we escalate our contributions to support a $19-billion-per-year cosmetic industry, buying everything from hair dye to skin tighteners. If we make it to seventy, cosmetic surgery (if it hasn't been employed yet) is almost certainly considered. And through it all, death—inevitable though it must be—is the one thing that we prefer not to contemplate.

There was a time, even in America, when people died at home. It still happens, perhaps with more frequency today than twenty years ago, but clinics, nursing homes, and hospitals are more typical send-off sites. Death at home seems somehow, well, unnatural.

From its late 1970s arrival on the scene, through the advanced symptomatic cases reported first in 1981, until widespread adoption of antiretroviral drugs in the late 1990s, the American AIDS community was dying. Members of this community—those who were HIV-positive—came in all shapes and sizes, in both genders and some in between, in various colors, races, and religions, from all economic and social groups. Mostly, we were gay white men under age fifty—leading to the fiction that only gay white men under age fifty got AIDS. But as my arrival in the community demonstrated, it wasn't being gay that bonded us, or being male. It was dying. Nobody was going to get out of this epidemic alive.

In school we learn how to add and subtract, how to read and write, how to recite the Pledge of Allegiance, how to behave in the sandbox. We do not learn how to die. I understand this. For many, it is a subject better left to the parents, to individual communities of choice, or to the silent, slow revelation of life. But after a few years in the AIDS community, I began to appreciate the lessons that come with the recognition that we will die. I began to recognize that some lessons simply must be taught out loud.

When Jefferson Davis High School in Montgomery, Alabama, invited me to speak in the fall of 1994, I told the assembled student body that "before you go on with your life, I wish you could have a sense of your own death."

Most of us come to our mid-teen years without any close brush with death. And it isn't only teenagers—many of your parents and other adults have so carefully avoided direct contact with death that they are still able to deny that it will enter their own lives.

But here's the cost of such denial: If we don't see that life is limited and, in some respects, terribly short, then we won't see the urgency of making a difference now, reaching out to care for others now, putting ourselves on the line now.

Teenagers will make a difference after they've finished school. Young adults will make a difference after they've married and settled down. Midlife adults will make a difference after the children are raised and the bills are paid. Older adults will make a difference when they are retired and have more time. Finally, we don't make a difference because it's too late . . . By failing to factor in death, we never really taste the importance of life, which is given to us only in the present.

This was, I think, the most positive spin I could put on death and dying.

Most of my experience with death, though, wasn't positive or valued. It found those I loved and destroyed them; what was left of them was shuffled away or burned. It settled over our homes and our minds, filling days with planning for the children when we'd be gone, haunting our nights with fears we could not always set aside. As I watched others who were farther down the road to AIDS, I saw in the most vivid details the shape of my own future: Nausea that couldn't be managed. Diarrhea that wouldn't be stopped. Wasting, dementia, bleeding, open sores, pain, pain, pain . . .

How was I ever going to manage this—especially with the children? I'd wondered about this from the moment of my diagnosis, but with time the question actually became more conspicuous and harder to face. The more I learned about my own AIDS, the more I realized that my greatest joy—being a mother with two small sons—was also my greatest problem.

IN THE WAKE OF the August 1992 speech in Houston, leaders of the AIDS community invited me in. I had neither betrayed nor embarrassed them, at least not too severely. I received invitations—mostly by fax

Faith

is the

ability **to live**

hopefully

without

the answers.

or phone or through mutual friends, in those days before e-mail was a fact of life—to join them at conferences and public events, in marches and walks and protests, in policy discussions and conventions. They even invited me to speak.

Looking back from here—where I'm two decades older—it's clear to me that some of those invitations were offered with mixed feelings. The sentiment within the AIDS community, with good reason, was that gay Americans were being killed and America didn't care. Attitudes toward dying gay men seemed to range from *That's too bad* to *That's what happens to you* to *You had it coming.* Stony silence on the part of policy makers, cabinet secretaries, and White House representatives, all of whom had volumes to say on everything else, yielded the inevitable conclusion by those with AIDS that all this dying was okay with the politicians. Some of the people who were actually doing the dying felt that my speech had provided cover for guilty Republicans in general and the White House in particular. For those approaching the end of life, and for those who loved them, I must have been hard to stomach.

I was another of the "victims" who could be embraced without the need to touch gay men. Members of Congress from both parties voted for AIDS funding named for Ryan White, the Indiana schoolboy everyone could love. But where were the Republicans when their constituents' gay sons died of AIDS and their obituaries spoke only of cancer? At least some of them were looking for another Kimberly Bergalis, the spectral victim wheeled into a Senate hearing room weeks before her death to give her testimony on how her dentist had, she said, infected her. Then along came Mary Fisher, with her father's credentials, her three strands of pearls, and her unwillingness to blast the president.

At the time, when I would get a whiff of such judgment against me, I was hurt and angered. My AIDS was as real as theirs. Their wasting and cancers would be no more vicious than mine. At least they—men—had barricades, and scream obscenities at the passing presidential motorcade. If someone didn't like it, so what: *What are they going to do, kill us?*

Speeches became the places I told the truth. Sometimes they may have sounded like descriptions of how I was coping. In fact, the speeches were themselves a means for coping, a way to identify the experience and express my feelings of fear, regret, satisfaction, hope, anger. Jeffrey Schmalz had said to me, "Feel the pain, and tell others. What else is there?" When working through a speech manuscript a day or two before a scheduled event, I would say to myself, almost in surprise, 'Hey, this is right! This is exactly right.' It was as if in the process of expressing some feeling or insight, I was able to discover it even for myself. My art was beginning to produce the same experience. I would start a piece not quite sure where it would end; along the way, I would discover what my soul had in mind.

Shadowing my speeches, as with everything in and related to the AIDS community, was the dying. If my own dying began as a project, it soon grew into an essential part of my identity. It was not only what I was doing, it was who I was becoming: a dying speaker, a dying woman, a dying mother. The exaggerated American fear of death may also produce an exaggerated sympathy for those who are dying, at least if we think they deserve better. Audiences who assembled to hear something pathetic from me were astounded when they heard humor. Some of them barely dared laugh. *Isn't she supposed to be dying?* they must have thought. The dying gave me a patina of heroism just for showing up, sounding upbeat, and telling the truth. So it wasn't all bad.

On the other hand, a downside of dying is that it discourages new romantic relationships. Dying is not sexy, and for most men, it's not part of what they're looking for in a relationship.

Maureen Dowd, now a columnist for the *New York Times*, filed a long magazine story on me in late 1994. It was one of the few times I stayed on the record when a journalist asked about my desire for a romantic partnership. I admitted that in the months following the diagnosis, I didn't "feel very sexual and sensuous." I knew post-diagnosis relationships were possible, but

the community I come from is not as welcoming for a woman with AIDS as the gay community is to itself. My world in dating and relationships is small to begin with: I'm divorced . . . a mom with two children, fairly independent. You add HIV to it and the pool of potential men goes down to practically nothing.

What I apparently did not say to Maureen, although it would have been true, is that I sometimes longed for a solid, intimate, fully romantic relationship. Perhaps I did tell her, and she protected me.

I wearied of being a single mother. I was lonesome. I wanted to be held, kissed, touched in all the ways that say, "You are beautiful, you are desirable, you are loved." Even with AIDS, even dying, I was still a woman.

I MET ARTHUR ASHE late in his life. He was already thin and sick when we were introduced, but his mind was undiminished; he was staggeringly wise. Where another athlete, Magic Johnson, brought power and laughter, Arthur Ashe brought a quiet, tough intellectualism. In every way possible, he exuded love for Jeanne, his wife—in her own right, a world-renowned photographer—and, as only a father could treasure a child, their daughter, Camera. And he hated AIDS.

Arthur had agreed to be the concluding speaker for a public lecture series at Salem State University in Massachusetts, but he died a month beforehand, in February 1993. At Jeanne's request and with the college's approval, I stood in for him.

The Salem State campus was only a few miles from the home of my former husband, Brian Campbell. Since our divorce, my conversations with Brian had been strained. We'd occasionally touch base to find a time when the boys could visit with him and, within moments, we'd be quarreling. I had some unresolved anger issues, and they were really unresolved, really angry, and really issues. But Brian wanted to see the boys while we were nearby; he said he'd like to hear me speak, too. We agreed that he would attend the lecture and visit the children there.

That evening, though I was speaking from a public podium, I spoke privately to my former husband. It wasn't the only time my audience assumed I was speaking generically, to a mythical "someone," when in fact I had a particular listener in mind. But this was different. This was Brian, who had coaxed me into becoming an artist, who had loved me into marriage, who had conceived one child and adopted another with me. This was the man who had left me with AIDS—but also with art and children.

Brian was somewhat desperately trying to quiet the boys when I came on stage for my introduction. Even in the cavernous auditorium, I found him instantly near the back. By the time I finished speaking, both boys were asleep and Brian was just looking at me from the shadows. He had heard me say things I needed him to hear.

*Death is not what **God** is really like.*

> *I want to say publicly what I've had a hard time saying privately: We can spend our lives in anger at a tainted needle . . . or an undetected virus in someone we loved. Or we can set aside the anger in favor of forgiveness, and move on . . .*
>
> *We can live our lives regretting the moment we were not careful; we can consume our children with our own guilt at leaving them; we can hate ourselves until there's nothing left worth saving. Or we can learn to forgive ourselves as well as others. This is neither pop psychology nor cheap grace; it is merely living out the ancient hope that we will one day learn how to pray, "Forgive us our debts . . ."*
>
> *If you need to hear a word of forgiveness, hear it now. The road is hard enough, and we will grow weak too soon. We must forgive even ourselves, reach out to take another's hand, and move on . . . And God give us strength.*

It was nothing less than grace that I was unaware of what those few hours in Salem, Massachusetts, would mean. They would be Brian's last cogent visit with our sons; two months later he would be dead.

In fact, it was mid-June when I headed to Brian's home because he was dying. Hank Murray, my AIDS doctor, had advised me, "Don't be afraid of death." I thought I would be fine, but I had never experienced anything like this before.

By the time I arrived, a bed had been set up for Brian in his living room so he could say good-bye to friends and family. We spent most of Friday evening (June 18) looking at pictures of the boys, talking about art, and remembering. When he finally drifted off that night, I lay next to him, watching, listening to his breathing, softly telling him things he did not hear and I'd never before said—about my fear of him, how much I missed him, why I could still love him.

Saturday was harder. Brian was disoriented, and I was frightened. When evening finally came, he fell asleep at last. Through the night— through the candlelight, the music, and the sound of his breathing— I watched. Near dawn he woke up in terror; I talked to him as gently as I could, saying, "I love you, Bri," and "I'll take care of the boys, don't worry," and "It's okay, Bri, you can let go now. It's enough. It's enough . . ." I wanted to be strong. I wanted to be unafraid of death.

Daylight came and, as if summoned by the sunshine, Brian left. It was Sunday, June 20, 1993. Father's Day.

IN BRIAN'S DYING, HE and I, aided especially by his nurse Manny Souza, found our way to acceptance and even to love. My anger was not ended so much as suppressed, but forgiveness made it more tolerable. My hours with Brian at his death were what I later called "a looking-glass experience," a mirror showing me the shape of my own future. In this, I shared an experience endured by hundreds of thousands of gay American men during the first fifteen years of the plague, an experience in which I was to participate more often than I want to recall. Time after time, condos intended for perfect dinner parties were converted into dimly lit hospices as one infected lover would become caregiver for the other.

In those days, gay men who died of AIDS knew exactly how and what they were going to suffer. A caravan of unheralded, often unpaid, sometimes unappreciated, and frequently heroic people cared for these men along this unknown road to AIDS. They taught me the meaning of courageous compassion—they were, for us, Frankl's men passing through the camps, giving away their last piece of bread.

IN 1992 WE HAD created the Family AIDS Network, a nonprofit organization dedicated to advocacy on behalf of families impacted by AIDS. During the years of dying, as my own experience with death grew inevitably deeper, an appreciation of the caregivers caught up in this epidemic led us to make them the focus of the Family AIDS Network's programs. Guided by the Honorable Steve Gunderson after he retired from the United States House of Representatives in 1996, the network profiled the impossible work done by the caregivers who tended the sick and dying. I can still name them, still see them, still hear their kind voices and sturdy confidence, still recall the price they paid in emotional and spiritual pain. Before the advent of life-extending medications, during the days when death waited impatiently at the end of every road to AIDS, these caregivers were the angels along a hard path to glory. They knew death in those days, and they knew community rejection. "The stigma and brutality toward those who are infected is a shameful legacy," I said in 1993. "I wish we could say it has ended, but we cannot. Therefore, I wish we could say communities have rallied against it, but we cannot. Therefore, the road continues to be hard and long."

We lived in those days, as did everyone in the AIDS community, with the inevitability of early death. We all had our own peculiar countdown, and we measured our progress toward our final days by watching "our numbers"—our T-cell counts, which inform us of our body's ability to fight off infection—drop past 600, 400, and 200 (AIDS!). When our numbers reached two, we named the cells Frick and Frack, a standing joke known in every corner of the American AIDS community.

I remembered all this clearly when I was told, recently, that I had cancer, and quite a bit of it. I remembered thinking, after my HIV diagnosis in 1991, *Okay, AIDS. And now I'll die.* Compare that to the experience of learning I had cancer: "Wow, that's an unhappy surprise."

The surgeon had delivered his woeful news in the tone of voice studied for such moments. I did not ask to hear it again. I got it. Perhaps a half-hour went by, maybe forty-five minutes, before my next thought: *Okay, so it's cancer. What's it going to take to fix it?*

I sounded like my father.

4

Healing

The night was full of diving and surfacing, dropping into sullen memories and rising to wakefulness. I gave up hope for sleep, padded to the coffee pot, and drank my way toward consciousness. Quietly I showered, brushed, dressed and slipped into the studio. Alone, before the sun rose, my hands began to show my eyes what I had feared, and loved, and longed for. In the stillness I realized that, almost against my will, it was returning: the inspiration to keep going, to stay alive, to make art again. My soul was inspired. Tuesday. It was Tuesday.

WHAT BROUGHT THE REPORTERS and the cameras, what made my story compelling at the 1992 Republican National Convention and elsewhere, was that I was dying. In the midst of a gay, male epidemic in which there was vast dying, I was a novelty: a dying Republican mother.

Between the moment I heard my HIV diagnosis and the moment I walked off the stage in Houston, I spent thirteen months coming to grips with dying. Having death not just up ahead but within sight changed everything. My future suddenly had a boundary line drawn through it. Even if death was years off, it was *only* years off—not decades, not a large fraction of a century. Ten seconds before my diagnosis, I was 40 or 50 percent of the way through my life; ten seconds after, I was 80 to 90 percent finished. I was virtually healthy, feeling well, dying. A darkness, a pall fell over what had previously been pure light: my time with Max and Zachary. From the moment the doctor, a stranger, said, "I'm sorry, it's positive," I knew I was leaving the boys. Not someday—someday soon.

When Brian grew ill and died in 1993, I reframed what I knew: I was going to leave them as orphans. I was living on what Paul Monette summed up in the two-word title of his memoir, *Borrowed Time*. Yet I didn't want my sons growing up in a morgue. If anything, after Brian's death, I focused on being more positive, more upbeat. They needed security, after all.

Some days I wished I could predict how long I had before the virus sickened me. If I knew precisely how long I could be a passable mother, I thought, then I could plan; I could organize. But all I knew with certainty was that at some not-too-distant future point, before Max needed to shave or Zack asked a girl to dance, I would become a burden, a hard-breathing shell—something I didn't want them to see.

When they were restless during the night, I'd take them to my bed. A few hours later, I'd open my eyes in the dawning sunlight, listen to their soft breathing, lightly finger their hair, and wonder, "So what's left? Six years, maybe seven? Maybe five? Maybe four?"

TWENTY-TWO YEARS BEFORE I learned I was AIDS-bound, Swiss psychiatrist Elisabeth Kübler-Ross gave the world her landmark book, *On Death & Dying*. With the dual gifts of science and empathy, she taught us that when facing death (or another profound trauma) most people go through five stages: denial, anger, bargaining, depression, and acceptance. Anyone facing death knows that she's probably right.

During my first few years of living with my diagnosis, I spent maybe a few weeks in denial, explaining to myself why it couldn't be true, why this was all just a misunderstanding. The test was a "false positive"—it happened all the time. I didn't allow myself much anger, although that was probably nothing but my own inability to acknowledge my own anger. And I don't recall bargaining or any depression—at least not then. In some respects, and imperfectly, I think I landed fairly quickly on the square marked *Acceptance*.

Psychiatrist Brian Weiss helped me enormously in coming to accept the realities. By "accept" I mean not just mumbling a begrudging "I have no choice, I'm going to die," but actually embracing the experience, discovering an "okay-ness" with the fact that AIDS was going to take me to an early grave. We were looking for what Brian calls "wellness," meaning that I could live contentedly, with a sense of purpose, not fighting the undeniable realities. With Brian's help, by mid- or late-1992 I could honestly say that, more often than not, I had moved from abhorrence to acceptance.

That didn't mean, of course, that I was going to let my life slip away from me. I remember hearing this story: A friend visiting W.C. Fields on his deathbed found the great comedian, who was famously agnostic, reading the Bible.

"My God, Bill, what are you doing?" asked the friend, shocked.

"Looking for a loophole," said Fields.

I laughed when I heard it, but I certainly identified with that sentiment.

What I struggled with most wasn't the dying, actually; it was the prospect of how I would die. I wanted to die healthy, like the blondes in the movies who are anything but invalids. They go on a romantic romp, displaying inexplicable energy and looking stunning. Then they bat their eyelashes a few times, sigh, and die. That seemed acceptable to me. The idea that I would spend a year or two fighting infections, sores, blemishes, boils, cancers, every form of gastric distress, and indescribable headaches—and that finally, looking skeletal and wishing it would all end, I would die when pneumonia suffocated me . . . this was less acceptable. I was teased by the possibility of wellness. I imagined healing.

Back then, the AIDS community was constantly abuzz with rumors of treatments that would fix symptoms if not causes, of cures that modern medicine had hidden from those suffering from this new disease. Especially within the gay community, distrust of the Establishment was bolstered by the belief that Republican power brokers and presidents seemed willing to watch, not act, as tens of thousands of gay Democrats died.

In the late 1980s the drug AZT had swept in, raising expectations and hopes for at least a stabilizing effect. For about two years, AZT was thought to be the redeemer. Physicians were cautious but, like their patients, hopeful. When the benefits of AZT began to wane, they increased the intensity of dosages, possibly even hastening death for some who overdosed on the drug. But at the time, while ACT UP (the advocacy group AIDS Coalition to Unleash Power) paraded in front of the White House and FDA hearings grew circuslike, AZT was the only pill on the shelf that looked like it mattered.

By 1990, hope tied to AZT was seen mostly as hype. Disillusionment swamped the AIDS community. Anger and frustration mingled with fear and the smell of death. Wellness was hard to find in this context, and the community went back to improbable searches for something, anything, that would kill the virus. Practically everyone in the AIDS community, including me, adopted some version of the "Why Not?" Theory: *If I'm going to die anyway, why not try something? Why not try anything?* It's what inspires parents of children with terminal disease to fly to Latin America for injections, or to Eastern Europe for surgeries, or to Italy for prayer. *Who knows?* they think in desperation. *Why not?*

In the first months after going public, I was deluged with "cures." Some came from friends or extended family members, who may not have had any faith in the suggested remedy but didn't want to be guilty of withholding what might have saved my life. After all, if people had known they only had to wash their hands with soap and hot water, millions of anguished parents would have raised their children, not buried them.

Some weeks, my mailbox was stuffed with proposals offering cures or wanting money to pay for studies to prove something worked. My fax machine whirred. The options were mind-boggling. Since the virus lurked in the bloodstream, infusions and transfusions were popular suggestions. Some required infusions of blood of other humans; one involved the blood and "serum" of cats. The "milk cure" suggested you pump goat's milk into your system. Hyperbaric chambers could cure you with pure, pressurized oxygen, and so could certain kinds of low-level radiation and low-spectrum light. How about a mixture of carrot and turnip juice that has been "known for centuries but blocked by the FDA"? Why not try putting your blood through a centrifuge to spin the virus to death? You could live on wild mushrooms, or bombard yourself with vitamins, or remove all fats from your diet, or add "the oil of a venomous snake." I heard it all: "I have a scarf that has been blessed by the yogi," and "The holy water in which this cloth has been dipped will save you," and "If you send just one hundred dollars, you will be cured." I'm still not sure what's more astounding: the range of quackery that showed up in my life or the fact that—quietly, usually alone, often late at night—I would sometimes wonder: *Who knows? Why not?*

When your prospects are grim, or worse than grim, you're ripe for the pickings, perfectly positioned to be duped by the false promise of a cure. You wonder because you cannot help wondering. You look at your children, measure how much time you have left, and open the envelope containing that day's goofy suggestion: wheat germ mixed with urine. (Okay, on that one, I knew "why not.")

Then there were requests for product endorsements. I could understand the pharmaceutical company's request for me to pitch its newest AIDS-related drug. I wasn't offended, but still I declined. And I didn't take offense, at least not much, at the repeated and fairly insistent request for me to endorse a manufacturer's primary money-maker: condoms. They offered me a choice of colors, textures, lubricants, strengths, and—with some obvious limitations—shapes. They were willing to give me rights of all kinds and a very nice paycheck. All they wanted in return was the right to use my name and face in their packaging and promotion. For weeks, I entertained friends and family with the suggestion that I'd soon be hawking my goods for a quarter in their local gas station restrooms. Ultimately, the condoms went the way of the wheat-germ-and-urine cure.

I actually had no interest in product endorsements and was rarely seduced by the zany cures. What held me back on endorsements was common sense. What held me back from outlandish cures was the same common sense and a second factor: fear of building false hope. I didn't want to repeat, privately, the AZT experience the greater community had shared—building expectations only to relive the death-sentence moment. If you allow yourself to build hope, you put yourself at terrible risk of pain.

In the middle of a plague, when everyone with your virus is sick and dying, the hope that *you* are the one who will not become desperately ill, that *you* will be the one who does not die, requires either great folly or great courage. Some days, I was courageous; some days, I just knew I was going to die.

MY FIRST AIDS DOCTOR was Henry "Hank" Murray. He is based in New York City, and I shared him with Arthur Ashe, among many others. After Arthur died, Hank took on increased responsibility for the Arthur Ashe Foundation. He continues to be a genius resource and a friend.

The same is true of Steve Grinspoon at Massachusetts General Hospital and Harvard Medical School. Steve is an endocrinologist and researcher who has led investigations and studies focused especially on women with HIV/AIDS, and I've been enthusiastic about his work since we met in the mid-1990s. Steve has become my reference point for all things metabolic and endocrine.

But to the question "Who's your doctor?" I have answered, for the past nineteen years, "Mike Saag at the University of Alabama at Birmingham." Every expert in the HIV/AIDS medical and scientific communities knows Michael S. Saag. Most people outside this relatively small audience do not. For a while, I thought we should make him famous everywhere. Now, more selfishly, I think keeping him to ourselves makes sense.

Mike is the doorway to every decision I make about illness, symptoms, medicine, and AIDS. Ironically, I might never have met him had it not been for my mother. Once I told her I was headed for AIDS, she began harping on me to "go see your cousin." Although I don't think Mike and I had ever met as adults, we share a common set of Louisville relatives, my grandparents Papaharry and Flohoney. In the summer of 1993, to satisfy Mother as much as myself, we went to Birmingham with my brother Phillip to meet Mike and hear his explanation of how HIV works in the human body. As it turned out, Mike was the first person who was able to explain it in simple, ordinary terms that we all understood. Not only that, but his research into how to counter HIV through antiretroviral (ARV) therapy was nothing short of groundbreaking.

On November 10, 1993, Mike sent me a warm letter suggesting that "we should sit down to discuss options for antiretroviral therapy." Today, ARV is standard protocol for anyone with HIV. It is the "cocktail" that first produced the so-called Lazarus effect as near-dead AIDS patients rose from their beds and walked. Mike was at least two years, maybe more, ahead of the curve in terms of science, medicine, and patient care. If I needed to name a single person responsible for my being alive today, it would be simple. It's Mike.

Before I met him, my stereotypical image of an AIDS researcher had been someone in a white lab coat, tucked away in a basement laboratory—someone slight, grey, quiet, and boring. On the contrary, Mike Saag invades a room like a happy hurricane. At six foot something and 200-plus pounds, he's prone to begin his formal presentations by singing (not particularly well) something from a Broadway comedy or a Monty Python movie. When he sings, he dances, and when he dances, he jiggles. The first time I heard him belt out pieces, with choreography, from *Robin Hood: Men in Tights*, I laughed until I wept.

Probably no story in my second book, *I'll Not Go Quietly*, has been quoted more often than this one about Mike Saag and his patient, Billy "The Boxer" Cox:

> *Billy Cox came out of his hospital bed in Birmingham, Alabama, to bring me a hug in Montgomery.*
>
> *I'd first met him a year earlier at the University of Alabama at Birmingham where I was visiting Michael Saag . . . Michael wanted me to meet Billy, to see his spunk and spirit. "Billy's the boxer in the ring," Michael once observed. "The doctors and nurses and medical staff, we're just the trainers in his corner. His friends and family are his fans, cheering him on."*

We must measure

the

value of our lives,

not

by life's length

but by

its DEPTH.

Now, a year later, I'd come to Montgomery to speak about community, about bridging gaps that divide us, about enabling us to live and die together. But what I said was not as eloquent as the events that soon played out in the life of Billy the Boxer and Cousin Michael.

Six weeks after he'd brought his hug to Montgomery—seven years, four months, and three days after testing positive for the AIDS virus— Bill Cox died. November 23, 1994.

On Billy's last day, Michael Saag was leaving town for a few days and stopped in just to say good-bye. When he heard Billy's labored breathing, he called the family together and told them the end was near. And then—as nurses and old friends and Billy's family crowded into the room, forming a remarkable community bound only by love for the boxer—Michael rested his head on Billy's chest and, unashamed before the crowd, sobbed, "I'm sorry, I'm sorry."

This is the sort of character Mike Saag brings to the fighting corner, and his patients become his partners in battling the disease. He refuses to accept the verdict of death, and he would not hear of my dying. Like Brian Weiss, Mike is passionate about healing in the sense of creating wellness and quality of life. He does not just throw pills at AIDS; he inspires hope.

I came to AIDS skeptical of physicians who like prescribing drugs. In my adolescence, when I was judged overweight, the family doctor recommended diet drugs to solve the problem. When the side effects kicked in—unnatural highs and sleeplessness—sleeping pills were prescribed. When sleeping pills left me drowsy, I got stimulants. The message was *Got a problem? Take a pill.* By the time AIDS found me, I had a jaundiced view of the pharmaceutical lifestyle.

Mike Saag's prescriptions were exercise, good diet, positive thinking, gobs of laughter—and pills. I was hesitant about the pills, but he insisted. "Birthdays are my business," he'd say. "This will work, I'm pretty sure of it." When I protested to Mike that I was tired, that the side effects were rotten, that the weight gains and the energy drains were ruining me, that I had a thousand good reasons to give up, he listened. And then he said, in the nicest possible way, "Let's stick with it for a little while longer."

For nearly two decades Mike Saag has been a force in my life, which in some ways puts him in the same category as my children. If I have lived at some moments *for* them, I have lived at some moments *because of* him. When, in the late 1990s, the battery of drugs I was taking left me constantly, miserably sick, I decided that it was time to take "a drug holiday"—I went off every medication Mike had prescribed and let myself feel well again for as long as possible. From my perspective, it was a decision to rediscover a life worth living, not just a life endured. From Mike's perspective, it was a calculated gamble he wouldn't endorse but reluctantly supported. I stayed off the drugs for about seven months, regained strength, and recovered joy.

Two things took me back to ARVs, with which, for all practical purposes, I've remained ever since. One, Mike had uncovered a new combination of therapies that he thought would have less debilitating side effects, so the holiday no longer had any real purpose. And two, my decision to stop therapy had gotten some media play. I was hearing from others that if I could stop the drugs and feel okay, they could stop too. I wrote letters, gave interviews, answered e-mail, and delivered speeches explaining that my decision was based only on my condition, not someone else's, and that stopping ARVs against medical advice could kill you. But the possibility that my decision would cost someone else their life terrified me. I went back on ARVs.

MIDWAY BETWEEN MY DIAGNOSIS with AIDS in 1991 and the discovery of my cancer in 2012 came an interesting moment in Denver in August 2003.

It had been a difficult summer. I wasn't feeling especially well: constantly tired, listless, disinterested in doing any serious work or play. But I'd agreed to serve on the Presidential Advisory Council on HIV/AIDS (PACHA) when named by President George W. Bush. His program for AIDS prevention and treatment in Africa—the United States President's Emergency Plan for AIDS Relief (PEPFAR)—had vastly improved on anything accomplished by any of his predecessors. It has saved lives by the millions. I will forever be grateful for this; President Bush remains a hero to many fighting AIDS in Africa, and justifiably so. By contrast, PACHA seemed marginal and ineffective—slow to comprehend the true issues and even slower to react.

My service on the Council was tortuous. It was, in my opinion, heavy on ideology and light on wisdom. PACHA was, for example, big on abstinence and silent on stigma. I finally wrote to my council colleagues in frustration:

As a woman who contracted AIDS in marriage, [I must point out that] a policy urging sexual abstinence—unless we intend to prohibit sexuality in marriage—would have done little to prevent my infection. By contrast, if there had been less stigma, less prejudice, less fear ([and] more acceptance, more inclusion, and more compassion), the factors that keep people from being tested would be diminished and my own risk would have been reduced.

I railed against policies that disseminated "the impression that to be gay is to be less than worthy of full human dignity and rights." The Council majority thanked me and ignored me. I was not having fun.

Two weeks after this skirmish with the Council, I was in Denver key-noting the annual conference of the National Association of People with AIDS (NAPWA). Here, speaking to a ballroom overflowing with people with AIDS, I could have fun.

> *As a person with AIDS, I need the unity of our community. As a woman with AIDS, enduring every side effect and drug-stimulated symptom known to the medical community, I need hope. And as a Republican with AIDS, God knows I need humor.*
>
> *Being a Republican has its advantages. Like you, I may wake every morning to that arsenal of pills and persistent nausea. But unlike many of you, I can wrap my arms around the cold base of a nearby stool knowing that, at that very moment, the Reverend Pat Robertson needs to admit that I am still a member of his party.*

I heard the roar of laughter, but my mind was focused on a strange twinge in my chest. I tried to ignore the feeling as I continued to speak, but once offstage I couldn't ignore it.

I was struggling to breathe. As soon as I was out of public view, I consulted with a local physician, also called Mike, and soon I was being admitted to a nearby hospital. It was first diagnosed as a minor heart attack. When the symptoms passed, everyone assumed it had been a one-time event—everyone except Mike. He ordered tests; he explored options. Finally he said, "Let's try a 'bubble echo' test." When it was done, I heard him announce with considerable satisfaction, "I knew it." The problem turned out to be a hole in my heart, something I'd probably carried since birth. With Mike's evidence in hand, one of his friends in Birmingham, a gifted surgeon who regularly performs cardiac surgery on infants, inserted a miniature "umbrella" through the hole in my heart, opened it so it would block the leakage, and closed me up.

This episode probably had nothing at all to do with AIDS. It reminded me that my health was not restricted to a collection of obstacles and con-cerns stemming from one particular disease—that wellness encompasses the entire physical system. In Mike's work to locate the source of my cardiac problem and the surgeon's services to repair my heart, healing and wellness were pursued through physical intervention. Healing would come through my body and radiate into my spirit. I am enormously and eternally grateful for their healing work.

But there is another form of healing from which I've gained immeasurably over these years, although I've said less about it thus far. For lack of a better term, I think of it as "spiritual healing."

I'm cautious in this territory, because it's land-mined with weird history, strange characters, and confusing language. The term *spiritual healing* suggests to some people think of a sweating Oral Roberts grabbing their heads and shouting, "Heal this sinner!" That's not what I have in mind—although I'll admit that, of such things, I've increasingly learned to say, *Who knows?* And in my more recent experiences with a man known as John of God—a man who has helped me to see life upside down—I've become wonderfully conscious of healing rooted not in pharmaceutical research but in love of service.

My mother has always been deeply spiritual. The shelves in her library groan under the weight of books on Eastern religions, metaphysics, and spiritual philosophies. I host my own modest version of this esoteric collection, including Brian Weiss's books and counseling, which are unabashedly founded on spiritual principles and beliefs. As Brian often says to me, "It's all about love." Both Mother's modeling and Brian's counseling have encouraged me to embrace spiritual healing.

Though I didn't realize it, I had been exposed to this type of spirituality and its healing role when I was first introduced to Alcoholics Anonymous (AA) at the Betty Ford Center. At the start I thought of AA as a self-help approach. Then I imagined it was a form of group psychology. Only when I got below the surface of the Twelve Steps did I realize that it is, as it says it is, a spiritual program. Its primary founder, Bill Wilson, developed the foundational teachings of AA after what he later described as a "white-light experience" of God. Of the Twelve Steps, half explicitly reference God. For AA members, Step Three is the point of no return at which we "made a decision to turn our will and our lives over to the care of God as we understood him." We stopped drinking, but we stay that way by continually seeking "through prayer and meditation to improve our conscious contact with God," such that we have "a spiritual awakening as a result of these [twelve] steps." The consequence of our spiritual awakening is a life of service to others. It is, wrote Bill Wilson, "all about love."

When I left the security of the Betty Ford Center and Parkside Lodge, I took with me the philosophy of AA and, therefore, a spirituality that's been seriously pressed but never broken. It taught me that healing comes when we set things right with others and put life in proper perspective, including seeing ourselves as servants, not masters. The spirituality I learned and adopted says that I am not in charge. I must accept what I cannot change, align my will with the will of God, and replace self-reliance with humility, gratitude, and service to others. How? One day at a time. This is wellness. This is healing. This is serenity.

It is my spiritual program that fuels my wrath at stigma and prejudice, because discrimination and cruelty are tools of illness and death. They grind us down, lacerate our sense of worthiness, stamp us as less than human and less than worthy. If I am the object of such scorn and I accept as true what is being said of me, I cannot heal. I will die before I die; I can never be well. I will forever bear the illness of shame and sorrow.

A gifted surgeon could repair my heart on a beautiful November morning in Alabama; he could make me, literally, better than new. What it will take to repair an American culture that damns people who love others of their own gender or who carry a virus they never wanted, I am not sure. But I believe this: We cannot as a culture, or as a nation, experience healing so long as we are driven by the values of anger, prejudice, and self-righteousness. We will never have wellness in our families or our communities if we harbor hatred in our souls.

IN THE HOURS AFTER I was diagnosed with cancer, I once again heard Betty Ford's distant voice ringing in my ears: "How are you going to use this to help other women?" The question reflected her belief that every life crisis, every illness, every grief is given to us so that we can use it for the good of others. It was a lesson she ingrained in all of us at the center, including a man named Willi.

I think of Willi now and again, as I thought of him when the Betty Ford Center was celebrating its tenth anniversary and I was invited to speak at the Alumni Dinner. "One special person wasn't able to be here tonight," I said that night.

But I want you to know his irreplaceable contribution to my life. I met him here, eight years ago.

"My name is Willi," he said, "and I'm an alcoholic." So began my odyssey with Willi. . . .

On the outside, you'd think—as I did at first—that Willi and I had nothing in common but alcohol. He [was] a black man; I, a white woman. He'd come from poverty; I'd come out of privilege. He was cool and confident; I felt awkward and uncertain. He was tough and strong; I was frightened of myself, not yet strong enough to be vulnerable. When he saw something good, he'd explode, "Thank God!" When he stumbled over something hard, he'd mutter, "Ya gotta struggle. . . ."

Being sober is wonderful. But Willi's no longer sober, because Willi's no longer alive. AIDS took him. . . .

I remember the day, Betty, you gritted your teeth at the surgeon's news. I heard you clear your throat and take the mic. When women across this nation dared not breathe the words breast cancer, *when they hung their heads in fear and shame—I watched you climb the nation's rooftop and proclaim life over death. In speaking the words, you inspired a world to hope. In setting the model, you drained the terror and stigma. You did it not once, but twice, conquering more than cancer and more than addiction; you conquered the evils that were killing us.*

Somewhere in the distance, if any of you would stand on your tiptoes and cup your ears, you could catch a glimpse of a most remarkable man. When the promises get hard to keep, you'll see him stretch out his arms to steady you and hear him say, "Ya gotta struggle." And when you end the day sober—"healthy, happy, and clean"—you may hear a quiet voice with a strangely familiar ring chucking in the darkness, "Thank God . . . thank God. . . ."

Healing is a gift. It comes, sometimes in health and sometimes in illness, to let us live in such a way that our lives matter. When we can end the day with a gratitude list that includes giving of ourselves to someone else, anyone else, we will have loved, and served, and mattered. No matter that death has drawn a boundary across our future. In that moment, we are well. Thank God.

5

I Am Woman

─────── SOUL TRUTH ───────

I was taught to be polite, proper. If someone gave me a gift, I wrote a note saying it was the best gift ever. When strangers came to our home, I assured them my parents couldn't wait to see them. Asked, "How did you get it?" for the 9,000th time, I smile through a well-rehearsed answer as if I liked the question. But here's the soul's truth: I hated the gift, hadn't asked my parents' opinion of their guests, and how I got it is none of your business. The soul's truth is good for sanity. Some days, it's even good for a giggle.

THE FIRST WORDS TO escape my lips when I was told I had cancer were "You've got to be kidding me." I wasn't terrified and I wasn't amused; I was merely astounded. It wasn't possible. I had noticed no symptoms. Some women have frightening family histories. Not me. I've heard women say, "Something in me just knew." Not me. When I heard the diagnosis, I was flat-out *Are-you-crazy? There-must-be-some-mistake!* shocked.

I had the opposite reaction days later when I woke up after the surgery. As the postsurgical anesthesia wore off, after my initial reaction of *This really hurts*, I looked down at my chest and thought, *Huh . . . they cut off my breasts*. I'd been told precisely what was going to happen, so there was no shock. It was just recognition, awareness—being able to see that, my goodness, that's just what they did.

With absolute affection and respect for men, I feel the need to say this: Not one of them truly understands a woman's relationship with her breasts. Our first decade or so we're living a little girl's life, fending off the boys who fancy our pudding or our Oreos at lunchtime, when suddenly we discover a little swelling, then a budding, and then the boys are looking at our chest instead of our lunch. What woman doesn't remember her first bra? When we experiment with dressing, we build an outfit around our breasts: cleavage or no cleavage? Modesty or flirtation? We spend a lifetime discovering sensitive spots and means of arousal. And what many of us treasure above all is that most sublime of human experiences, which is absolutely restricted to women: cuddling an infant whose lips purse to suckle at our breast.

If we live long enough, we discover that breasts were created to give meaning to the word *sag*. American women invest more than $1 billion a year on surgeries, lotions, undergarments, and exercises designed to improve the look of our breasts. American men invest several billion more looking at our breasts in magazines, films, and videos, and now on the Internet. We are a society obsessed with the female form—the *perfect* female form—and we learn from an early age that breasts are essential to our identity as women.

Gloria Steinem's *Revolution from Within* contains a critical lesson on "the importance of unlearning." Women, says Steinem, need to unlearn those social definitions of ourselves that add up to our sense of being something less than men. The first trick after my surgery was to remind myself that I was no less a woman for the loss of my breasts.

The definition of "the ideal woman" during my 1950s childhood and my 1960s emergence into adulthood was a creature of beauty. Brains were optional; breasts were necessary. And in that one comparison—of our chests to our capabilities—a huge part of my struggle from adolescence through early adulthood could be defined. I wrestled with addictive behaviors and weight gains, habits that were mutually supportive: If you're overweight, you can take pills. What I really wanted, however, was affirmation that I was as good as the next person, that it was neither my father's power nor my bosom that kept me employed. When I was denied equal pay with the men doing my job at the White House, the explanation given to me was, and I quote, "You're a girl" (read: "You're less than").

By the time I'd become an artist and a mother, I had effectively unlearned my sense of being less than men simply because I am a woman. On the contrary, I felt confident and happy. My work as a professional artist was solid, and I was nothing short of ecstatic at being a mother. I was a woman expanding her horizons, continuing on the path of spiritual growth that had begun in the Betty Ford Center and was now nurtured by times with Brian Weiss and healthy friends. Being a woman was essential to being the person I knew myself to be, and it was good.

The surgery had brought me considerable pain and taken away my breasts. I did not yet know what other treatments lay ahead. Still, I did not find myself in a new place of fear; it did not occur to me that I would be rejected, or labeled, or even made to feel unfeminine. I knew that I had been dealing already with that fear for more than two decades; it couldn't be avoided if you are a woman with AIDS in America. In one of life's ironic twists—or perhaps it was one of those improbable acts of grace— the first disease offered me a point of comparison with the second disease. Compared to my emotional struggle with the stigma of AIDS, my experience with cancer was almost entirely a physical one. This contrast enabled me to say, while staring at my vacant chest, "If we can get rid of how much this hurts, I can get back to my studio."

AFTER ELIZABETH GLASER DIED in 1994, there were few well-recognized women with AIDS in America. Infection was becoming rampant among women, but research, treatment, and media coverage were missing in action.

My memoir, *My Name Is Mary*, was published in 1995. By then my story had been told and retold; I wasn't news anymore. The gay community was dying; those who hadn't died were exhausted and often sick. The advent of ARVs, and misimpressions about Magic Johnson's message, led to a widely held impression that AIDS had been cured. The Clinton White House was gifted at spinning positive stories on AIDS, including the 1997 message that infections in the United States had "plateaued." That American infections were at an all-time high didn't make the administration's story; that they were "flat" was all that mattered, despite the unacceptable altitude of that figure.

By this time I had moved to Nyack, north of New York City, to spend more and quieter time with the boys, to work in my studio, and to open a small gallery. Beginning even earlier, and increasing slightly month by month, I was coping with infections and side effects of the new drugs. But there had been little research involving women in the drug development and trials. I *was* the research for my own case, and I felt like a sick guinea pig.

In the lead-up to 1998's World AIDS Day (December 1), I noticed that the *New York Daily News* had produced a special supplement dealing with AIDS, and it focused on women. I was surprised to spot a familiar photograph under the headline women in crisis—and even more stunned to read the caption: *the late Mary Fisher, AIDS activist*. True, I hadn't been feeling well, but this was over the top.

I knew my mother would be irritated that I had not mentioned my death to her. Anytime I was splashed in the papers, she'd call and complain, "Mary, I'm always the last to know." I sent her the *Daily News* piece without comment, and she called me moments after she read it. She had no complaint, just motherly sympathy: "This is going to make it very difficult for you to get dates, Mary."

Mother was right. As a woman living with the HIV cloud hanging over my head, I was already familiar with that challenge.

MORE THAN FOUR YEARS earlier, in June 1994, Duke University had hosted a medical education conference for physicians and other health care providers that focused on women and AIDS. It gave me an opportunity, in the conference keynote, to speak honestly about issues being faced by women across the country:

> *I cannot count the number of times I've been told variations of the following story: An ordinary woman—you, me, your wife, one of our friends—goes to an ordinary physician. The woman is in her twenties or thirties or forties. She's lived an average life with all the average joys and crises, and a perfectly average number of public triumphs and private intimacies. Having reviewed her life, on one hand, and having scanned the American HIV statistics on the other, she says to her physician, "Maybe I should have a test for AIDS." And she hears the response, "You don't need an AIDS test. You're not* that *kind of woman."*

Days before the Duke conference opened in North Carolina, mothers with AIDS in two different states were forced to turn over their children to state child protection agencies. Prejudice and the AIDS mythology had become so prevalent, and protests had become so muted, that insanity was having its way with public policy. The rationale was entirely irrational: Any woman capable of being infected with the virus that causes AIDS was demonstrably incapable of competent parenting.

I don't believe any mother with AIDS in America missed the point. This hostile environment created another barrier to testing for women who had been at risk. And it taught us what we'd lost when we gained the virus: our womanhood. Unlike the community of gay men, who had formed their own networks and created their own systems of intervention and care, we were tied together by nothing more than the virus. We were, I said at Duke,

> *a community of women: young and old, black and brown and white, gay and straight, rich and poor, Republican and Democrat. We are women, living with a disease [that] our society defines according to its judgment of gay men. We are women, living largely in silence out of fear that we will lose not only dignity, but employment; not only insurance, but our children.*
>
> *I was raised to think of the ideal woman as someone of great virtue. To be feminine is to be pure. And society tells me that to have AIDS is to be dirty.*

I was trained to think of the ideal woman as someone of great beauty. To be feminine is to be desirable. And society tells me that AIDS is repulsive.

I am a mother, divorced, widowed, and embarrassed to say in public that I long to be held by someone who wants to hold a woman. I wonder how many times I've wondered if it is really true that AIDS has made me, literally, untouchable.

By the time Duke had gathered its audience, U.S. statistics were showing—even though the media was not reporting—that most American infections were resulting from heterosexual transmissions. Half of the infections were in people under the age of twenty-five; one out of four was in people under the age of twenty. "If you want to find AIDS, go looking among your children," I told a group in the Midwest, "because that's what the virus has done."

In heterosexual transmission, the risk has typically been greatest for women because of our anatomy. During sexual intercourse, the exchange of bodily fluids is primarily (although not exclusively) from male to female. Nothing exotic or rough needs to happen for tiny fissures and tears to be caused in the delicate tissue surrounding the vagina, or in the mouth or anus, and a tiny opening is more than enough to admit the virus.

But all this knowledge of statistics, anatomy, and physiology had little impact on public perspectives and public policy. Year after year, the Centers for Disease Control would report the rising incidence of AIDS among women. And time after time, I would sit with the head of the National Institute of Health's AIDS programs, asking why there wasn't more research being done on women, and I would be told, "Mary, we don't have any older women patients."

Of course they didn't have older women patients. Women weren't being treated because they didn't know they had AIDS—because they weren't getting tested. What woman in her right mind would get tested for a disease that, if you have it, means you are a tramp, a moral deviant? On top of all the economic and social barriers to testing, especially for women of color and women in poverty, American women avoided testing because of the overwhelming stigma associated with AIDS. This meant that we learned women had AIDS most reliably when they were admitted to hospitals because of other diagnoses, and usually when it was too late to be saved. The quickest, surest way for an American woman to be diagnosed with AIDS in 1994 was to die of it.

The data in 2012 is scarcely more encouraging. Somewhere between 1.2 million and 1.5 million Americans carry the AIDS virus; perhaps one-third of them are women. The imbalance toward men is historical: More men came first. But with time, new infections, and new deaths, women make up a greater and greater percentage of those with AIDS. New infection rates are about evenly divided between men and women. Of all those infected, 20 percent do not know they have the virus. Of those who do know, nearly half are receiving either inadequate treatment or no treatment at all.

The great leap forward in treating AIDS over the past thirty years has been in mother-to-child (perinatal) transmission. If women are tested and found to be positive, and if they are then or subsequently become pregnant, relatively small and inexpensive doses of available medicines even late into their pregnancies will practically guarantee that their children are born virus-free. All that's needed is a tiny bit of medicine—and the timely knowledge those women gain when they are tested.

Unfortunately, when our culture teaches women with AIDS that they are unworthy trollops, and when it threatens a woman with loss of her dignity and her children, it instills a terror that keeps women from being tested and punishes those who know they are HIV-positive with self-loathing and fear. I give a speech to a thousand people and, afterward, a dozen women will ask if they can speak to me privately. In the quiet of an anteroom or the shadows behind a stage, they will pour out their diagnosis in a flood of emotion and tears. Though the details vary, it is always the same story: While the virus assaults their bodies, the stigma assaults their souls. They do not have a physician they can trust. There is no clinic that speaks their language. They have no way to be treated without insurance. The only thing they do know with absolute certainty is terror.

In 2001 the renowned CBS program *60 Minutes* decided to do a segment on AIDS in America and, as a starting point, interviewed award-winning dramatist and activist Larry Kramer. The producers wanted to talk to a woman, and Larry persuaded me to be interviewed. I protested first to Larry and then to the producers: What they needed was fresh faces and new voices, not another shot of "that woman who spoke at that convention." Finally, one of the producers told me the truth: They had already tried to convince a dozen women with AIDS to come on-camera. All had said no.

"Isn't that exactly the story you need to tell?" I asked, frustrated. "Can't you explain that all the women you approached were too terrified, too intimidated, too frozen by their own fears?"

"Yes," said one of the younger producers. Fear was the story, all right. But what the program really needed was film.

I could hardly blame those women for balking at going on camera. I had chosen to go public mostly because of my children, so they would need neither to hide the truth nor to fear it. But now they were older, and I was sicker, and having the media review our private lives didn't seem appealing at all. Not one bit. But somebody needed to say something.

I did the interview.

I'M NOT SURE WHY I'd always wanted to be a mother. I actually believed I would have a bunch of kids—"a dozen," I used to say when asked if I'd like to have a child someday. Maybe I wanted a chance to be as good as my mother was to me, or even to improve on the model. I always enjoyed infants and other people's children; maybe it was envy. But I think it was a more basic urge—it was more about life than anything else. Something about the idea of giving life to another human being, and then nurturing that life, stirred both my hopes and my hormones. I simply wanted to be a mother. And when I conceived Max and knew he was growing within me, already I felt complete in a way I'd never before experienced.

The truth is, of course, that parenting comes with its own perils. I've visited most of them. When Max and Zack were very young, and usually when I was on a trip somewhere, one of them would, for example, put his head through the glass door in the kitchen or fall from a tree and break an arm. I'd get a call from the babysitter that would begin, "Let me say first that everyone is going to live . . ."

Of course, the trials of my sons' early childhood paled in comparison to those of their adolescence. I am convinced that they tried out every possible form of bad decision making. At the time I could hardly believe it, but the evidence was overwhelming. You name the category, and they'd find a way to turn it into a raging crisis filled with hostility and misunderstanding. School was reduced to a place they couldn't play video games for a fixed number of hours each day. Resentment was keen and loud. Curfews were set and violated. Despite my willingness to share with them the lessons of my mistakes, they insisted on learning from their own.

Max was moving into his midteens, and Zack was trailing him by two years, when the life-prolonging drugs that had been prescribed for me began taking their worst toll. Side effects, including a nearly constant flirtation with depression, took over my life. As the boys found the creativity to explore every bad idea that popped into their heads, I was retreating to my bed with nausea, cramps, headaches, and a *Woe is me!* attitude.

Being a single parent made all this no easier, and I confess that my anger with Brian did not stop at his grave. On more than a few nights, as I waited to hear whether this was the time some weird antic had actually killed one of the boys, I spoke to Brian in a tone of voice that should have easily reached him, wherever he is. What I said does not belong in a book.

How Max and Zachary could emerge from such a rocky adolescence and become the young men they are today baffles me. Cute toddlers turned into adolescent strangers who have now been transformed into lovely human beings. The only consistent line through all this, as near as I can tell, is that from beginning to end, I was their mother and they were my children. When, on their own initiative, each of our sons decided to change his name from Campbell to Fisher, I felt rewarded for having stayed the course. If we struggled with one another (and we did), we also loved one another—consistently and profoundly. I thank God that I was sober for their growing years. Had I lacked this one gift, I would've been unable to recognize and appreciate all the other gifts.

I do recognize, every time I review the years of my AIDS so far, that it's truly a family disease. Try as I did to protect the boys, what I was doing in public and saying in the media seeped into our home and into their lives. For a while, I thought that I was shielding them from the realities, that despite Brian's death and my illness we were living a "normal" life, whatever that might be. But now and then, evidence to the contrary would appear. I'd been deluding myself by thinking Zachary hadn't noticed my lonesomeness or felt his own. "I know how we can get another Daddy," he announced confidently one evening when he was five.

"Really?" I said, not sure I wanted to know what he had in mind.

"You just put on your pretty dress with your makeup, and you go out," he said. Zack, I realized, had survived the adoption, the divorce, and the AIDS, but he'd noticed the pain we were all living with. He had lost his father. Twice.

Max was eight when he asked a writer friend of mine to visit with him . . . alone. I wasn't allowed to listen in. After an hour or so, they ended their conversation, and neither said anything to me. But a few days later Max produced a "speech" the two of them had built together. I will never, ever forget the first time I read it:

When my Mom comes to say, "Good night" to me, she sits on the edge of my bed. After she's smoothed the covers for a minute, she bends over to kiss me goodnight and says, "Sleep with the angels, Max." And then she goes downstairs.

Sometimes it's hard to sleep, so I just think about things that happened during the day: the soccer ball I kicked. The spelling word I got wrong. Why I slammed the door. Or why I pushed my brother, Zack.

And when I think about all these things, sometimes I wish things were different. I wish that all the people in the world would live and not get sick. I wish all the children would grow all the way up. I wish parents would stay a long time. I wish everyone would last to be old people, about 120 years old. I wish all the people would take care of sick people and be nice to them.

Sometimes, when I shut my eyes very, very tightly, and I hold my breath so I'm very quiet, I see my Daddy again. I miss him a lot. He had AIDS and he died.

But in bed with my eyes squeezed shut, sometimes I can still see him running across the beach, lifting a blue-and-red-and-pink kite with a humongous tail, and finally letting it go up, up, up into the wind. This isn't a dream because the kite is real. Dad bought it for us and he painted it because he's an artist.

Sometimes when I see my Daddy like this, I think maybe I'm dreaming. Even in a dream, I want to ask him what he did while he was gone, after he died. But he doesn't answer. It doesn't matter though. Because mainly I just want to tell him that I still love him.

I love my Mom too, because she's the bestest Mommy in the world. She's really funny, and she makes me laugh a lot. I like it when she's

*alone with me, and she doesn't talk on the telephone, and I have her
all to myself.*

*I don't have to dream about Mom because she's right here. And I
don't have to wish much for her either. Because she already loves me.*

*My Mom says that I'm her wish. Maybe. But sometimes I worry.
When I worry, I wish my Mom didn't have AIDS.*

*But if she gets really sick, like my Dad did, I'll take care of her. And
I'll dream that nobody will die of AIDS anymore, ever again. And
then I'll make a very, very, very big wish for my Mom....*

We've come so far since Max's letter. My sons have become hand-
some, loving men, and I've moved from measuring the dimensions of my
grave to calculating bedroom space for future grandchildren.

When they were lurching through their acting-out years, hitting every
wall they could find and driving me to distraction, I would occasionally
say to them, "I know everything you're trying to get away with." I'd prove
my point by telling them what they assumed I did not know, and when
they'd ask how I'd found out about it, I'd say, "You can't hide anything
from me, because I'm your mother and I love you."

Looking back through the mists of our growing older together, hearing again the angry words when our trust had been broken and feeling
again the tender hugs when our hearts had been broken, I realize this was
true on both sides of our relationship. They couldn't hide their behaviors
from me, but I couldn't hide anything—the pain, the lonesomeness, the
stigma, or the sickness—from them either, because they're my sons and
they love me.

A UNITED STATES SENATOR once argued on the floor of the
Senate that people with AIDS shouldn't be allowed into the United
States He was defending a ban on any visitor who was HIV-positive, a
ban that was in place from the Reagan years until it was lifted by the
Obama Administration. The senator had in mind refugees and immigrants from Africa, the Caribbean, and elsewhere—many of whom were
women who, like me, had unknowingly been infected by their husbands. The argument is a hurtful one, but it was even more so because

just moments earlier, he had given me a wonderful hug and borrowed my large red-ribbon awareness pin.

I had just settled into the Vice President's senate office when the senator appeared on the television screen. His speech led to this conclusion: We don't allow infected fruit to come into the country, so why would we let infected people in?

Nearly three years later, I was at the 1996 Republican National Convention in San Diego. I'd had a mostly sleepless night, and I was in the hotel restaurant looking for a table where I could have a quiet breakfast. I heard "Mary!" and turned to see this very same senator motioning me to join him. It was too late to refuse him, so I sat down.

Once situated, I couldn't resist asking why he'd said what he'd said. At first he didn't recall the remark. When I reminded him, he defended it by "putting it in context" for me. Finally, seeing my skepticism, he leaned over and whispered, "Oh, Mary, you know—you're just not like the rest of those people."

Perhaps he meant to be kind, but this was the cruelest cut of all. Because I *am* like those other people—*exactly* like them. Just as being a woman doesn't separate me from the men, gay or straight, who must live and die with AIDS, being white doesn't separate me from my black sisters who share my virus, my side effects, my dread for what will be said or done to my children, my diminished hopes and daily fears. Nothing makes "blood relatives" out of people like sharing a virus in your bloodstream, a virus that wants to kill you. *Not like them?* I am *one of them*!

I knew then, knew in my bones, that this was true—that I was one with these women whose home is halfway around the world. But it wasn't until I'd spent time in Africa that the truth became real to me. It is a terrible irony—that only thousands of miles away, in an environment utterly unfamiliar to me, could I experience the fellowship, the community that I had sought so desperately in the United States.

Being in Africa is an uplifting experience for me because I am surrounded by so many other women with AIDS that here, in this place, I am not the freak.

In Africa, I feel an overwhelming unity with every person who is struggling with AIDS. When I am in the clinics or the hospices or the support groups, when I am with the other HIV-positive women and men and children—we have an instant bond, a relentless connection. We hug because we know how deeply we need one another. We sing and laugh and dance because we know that songs bring hope, and laughter brings health, and dancing brings our bodies to life.

Among the AIDS-infected women of Zambia, I have experienced an acceptance that has left me breathless, longing to be back with them when I am away. The first time I stood among them and said, "Yes, I understand, I also have AIDS," we discovered that we were sisters in a single family.

When all the surgeries and treatments for my cancer are in the past, I'll be more than ready to be back among the women who survived genocide in Rwanda, who were raped, mutilated, and infected with AIDS. Their bodies were hacked with field machetes, their arms and legs and parts of their faces lopped off. Somehow they survived—not only physically but emotionally, spiritually. I remember especially the women who spoke of having their breasts cut off, of being left to die in agony. They were surprised when I told them I had AIDS, when they realized we had that in common. I could surprise them again.

6

Hiding From the Anger

——————— SOUL SPECTRUM ———————

Every color in the rainbow could decorate
some aspect of my soul. I feel the cool green
of a morning garden, the brilliant blues of a
Sedona sky, the goofy orange of Halloween
pumpkins. My soul goes everywhere, and
everywhere on the spectrum there is a color.
Last week, I was holding a dying infant while
remembering the politician who told me,
"AIDS isn't my issue." I saw red. I saw it in
bloody scarlet.

———————————————————————

IT FEELS NEARLY DERANGED to say this, but if I had died on schedule, sometime around 1999 or 2000, I never would have needed to deal with anger. I could have just taken it to the grave, as I imagine generations of women before me have done. Although illness has no advantage over health, perhaps in this single way, dying holds an advantage over living.

I'm grateful to feel well today and to be alive, and avoiding my own anger came with its own costs. But I have known all my life that someone, somewhere, at some time before I arrived, crafted a social rule: Men can be angry and express their anger—it even makes them more masculine—but angry women are "bitches."

For the first three or four decades of my life, the messages I heard as a little girl, then as an adolescent, and finally as an adult were consistent: Anger makes men strong and aggressive. Anger makes women ugly and vindictive. For men, it's a naturally good thing. In women, it's a nasty trait.

I was not a temper-tantrum kind of child. I suffered no incidents of brutal abuse that I would repress into adulthood when it could explode in justifiable, or at least understandable, rage. I don't recall expressing anger over anything as a child, even though my younger brother, Phillip, claims I had a habit of kicking him, hard, in the shins. (I joyfully tell him that I was administering much-needed discipline because I loved him.) I wasn't an angry teenager or a rebellious young adult. If I liked James Dean–type characters, I didn't date many of them; I tended to go out with people I could bring home. I was never violent. I never got tattoos in places my parents wouldn't see. I was a pleaser. I wanted you to be happy—almost regardless of who "you" was. Even now, taking up the topic of my anger makes me a little queasy.

Which leads, of course, to the point: Anger has been a challenge in my life. I didn't like it, so I didn't admit it—not as a child, nor as a young adult, nor even well into my fifties. I have a stack of published interviews from the period of 1992 through 1996 in which I was asked repeatedly, "Aren't you *angry*?" Sometimes the questioner was thinking about my marriage and the fact that Brian had infected me with AIDS. Sometimes it was a broader question about generic anger at having the virus, or about anger at national policies that seemed inadequate or even degrading. But no matter what the truth had been about Brian's actions or some president's inactions, in these interviews I was mostly dismissive of the issue. I typically waved aside queries about being angry.

If I couldn't avoid the question, I had three stock answers to "Aren't you angry?" and all of them were *No*. No, I'm not angry, because I don't want my children to grow up in a house full of anger. No, I'm not angry, because we're all doing the best we can. And no, I'm not angry, because it wouldn't do any good. When pestered about my art, and what some critics took to be expressions of anger there, I would say that any interpretation was in the eye of the beholder. People will see what they bring. If they're angry, they'll see anger.

The first time I was nose-to-nose with my own anger, where I couldn't successfully evade or deny it, was at the Betty Ford Center. Even there, however, anger was just one more obstacle, one issue among many. That I felt or had preserved some anger mattered to me, but it wasn't a staggering discovery or breathtaking admission. I was at the Center in the mid-1980s, before I knew AIDS intimately, before cancer, and before I had fully learned to trust my own feelings or developed any ability to manage them. I came away from the Betty Ford Center recognizing that maybe I was harboring some resentments that could rise to the level of anger. Maybe.

In the six years between my recovery from addiction and my diagnosis with AIDS, I was increasingly conscious of what I was experiencing, of how to manage both the good and the not-so-good experiences, of how to identify feelings and respond to them appropriately. I learned, as the Twelve-Step program advises, how to accept what I could not change. These were years of growth as an artist, growth in self-expression, and growth in my awareness of being a competent woman. I married, and I became a mother not once but twice, both times intentionally and with great joy. Whatever else I could say about these years, they were certainly not angry.

Then came the HIV diagnosis, and I was instantly immersed in a seething sea of anger all around me and deep within me. Protesters wailed and street violence raged. When I watched the evening news, my stomach spun into knots. The world of AIDS was a world of anger, and I had no idea how to find a place for myself amid all that anger. I'd been in Detroit when the city had burned a quarter century earlier, the fires fueled by racial tensions and inequities, but those riots had been "theirs," not mine. This was different. In ways I could neither express nor deny, the anger of gay men wasting to death in front of the White House—and giving the finger to the media cameras—was, shockingly, my own.

"I'LL BE ANGRY FOR you." Interesting that these are among the words I remember most clearly. They were spoken by President Ford the day I told him Brian had infected me with the AIDS virus.

It was midmorning. I'd already had time with Mrs. Ford, explaining my visit was more than "just dropping by" their Colorado home. The

COMMUNITY

is a

fragile creature

and we are called

to **nurture** it,

to help it grow

vigorously

and **GROW STRONG.**

president was smoking a favorite pipe, reading a report of some kind. He hugged me, saw that something was wrong, and asked me about it. I told him the story. Even before I'd finished, I could see that his response was wrath. He didn't shout, but he invoked Brian's name in seriously unflattering tones. He was angry. A few years later I described sitting with Mrs. Ford and waiting for the president to say something:

> *When he walked back toward us, I saw that he was visibly angry. His fists were clenched; his face was red; his hands were shaking when he tried to light his pipe. I was worried. The president famous for never losing his temper in public, for being the calm negotiator of thousands of bills in Congress before coming to the White House, was furious. Finally he said it: "I'm angry, very angry." He was angry with Brian, angry with AIDS, angry with his own helplessness. "I'm not angry with you, dear," he said, "but aren't you angry yourself?"*
>
> *I said something like, "Anger isn't a very good emotion for me with the boys right now. They probably got enough of it with the divorce."*
>
> *"Okay," he said, "I'll be angry for you."*

President Ford acknowledged my reluctance to be angry at having been betrayed, but his acknowledgment wasn't tantamount to approval. He gave no hint of letting go of his own anger. Looking back across twenty years of growth, I find I'm more grateful for that today than I was then. I've learned to value the power of truth, also about our emotions. His honest anger reflected that (among other things) he cared.

The simple truth I was reluctant to confront for many years is this: I have anger. I was, and I still am, angry at Brian. I'm angry that he lied to me. Either he didn't take the AIDS tests he said he'd taken, or he did take the tests but misled me about the results. He was suffering from full-blown AIDS before he told me he'd been diagnosed. He must have known earlier. Despite what he knew, he was willing to play around with my life, putting me at risk with a wanton disregard that was criminal. And when I think of how Brian risked Max's health and his life, I seethe. Even now, my breathing shortens and my blood pressure climbs.

If I've learned something about my anger, I've also recognized more of my own responsibility. I can't assign all the blame for my infection on

Brian: I knew about his personal history, his risky drug use, his fast-and-loose lifestyle, the friends with whom we hung out, and the dangers that lived in his neighborhood when I met him. What I knew was enough to induce anyone to press for answers, but I never asked for them. I wasn't completely stupid, just naïve and trusting. The dangers must have occurred to me, but I preferred being ignorant to being unhappy. I have to accept my own responsibility for how I've lived my life, including my life with Brian.

My "other Brian"—Dr. Brian Weiss—continually and persuasively helped me focus during the years of 1991 and '92 on both my responsibility and my anger. I needed to consider not only how I felt but also what I was called to do. He was certain that, if I had the gifts of an artist, then my art would be a means by which I would communicate a bigger, bolder, broader message to the world. He persisted in saying that at the core of my message would be love. He was not being simplistic or Pollyannaish. He was convinced of this truth, and he was very convincing.

When I told him I was HIV-positive as a result of loving and trusting my husband, without breaking stride Brian Weiss spoke of a higher love and a bolder trust. Having AIDS changed how the message might be packaged, how my life would be a testimony, but it was still all about love and service. His philosophy and his therapy were pure Betty Ford. As I came through that first year of living with my diagnosis, he encouraged me to create a place within myself for forgiveness despite the anger. I could be angry, he explained, and still be forgiving. Anger is an emotion, but forgiveness is a choice, a decision, and one that affirms love in the face of anger.

As weeks became months, and months morphed into years, my health began to slip—not always dramatically, but noticeably. In 1994 I missed my first big public event, a speech, owing to illness. My energy had faded, and the children were older and needed more attention, more time. I couldn't do everything I'd done when I first went public. I had my hands full dealing with my own life, figuring out the best place for the children to live if I couldn't care for them, trying to arrange affairs so that, no matter what, Max and Zack could have lives as nearly normal as possible. Dealing with the goblins of internalized anger was not my top priority and would have been a dubious luxury.

I wasn't lying when I told all those interviewers that I didn't want my children growing up in an angry household. I wanted love, not anger, to define our family and, in those first years, the time they might have with their father—especially as it became clear that this time would be short. And I knew that where my former husband was, I was heading. Trying to live a life molded by as much affection as possible seemed reasonable. But the anger was still there, lurking, building explosive pressure. I remember moments of fearing my own anger, worrying that if it ever started to seep out, it would become an unstoppable rage. I could admit to other emotions. I expressed hurt, had no problem acknowledging grief, spoke of pain and loss. But anger stayed just out of range. I was convinced I could keep it packaged and take it with me when I left.

I might also have told both the interviewers and myself a harder, deeper truth if I had fully recognized it at the time: I still loved Brian. The separation had been hard, and the divorce had been terrorizing. Part of my defense against him had become not admitting I might still love him. But this was the man who'd taught me how to hold a brush in the studio, who'd encouraged me to risk saying, "I'll be an artist." We had worked together, played together, wept together, laughed together, conceived together. However ironic it may seem, the fact that we shared the AIDS virus somehow drew us closer. Lying with him in his dying hours, I was lying down with my own future. Divorce may draw a line, leaving a scarred *before* and a harsh *after*, but it does not cauterize love. It's not that clear-cut.

Brian Weiss had been right: I *could* be angry and still choose forgiveness. And in that choice I could find important ways in which I could love Brian again. Loving in the face of anger was not as hard as I may have wanted it to be.

PERSONAL BETRAYAL LEAVES AN anger that is hard and vexing. It longs for revenge. It dominates our emotions and tips us toward fury, self-pity, and self-righteousness. If we are emotionally healthy, we recognize that we don't want this anger to guide our thinking, shape our personalities, or define our relationships. But it can, and sometimes it does.

Denying the reality of such anger isn't healthy either. The truth is, a child who has been abused *ought* to feel anger toward his abuser. A woman raped, a neighbor slandered, a family shattered by a drunk driver—all have not only the right but probably the need to be angry and to express that anger.

I had swallowed an ounce of pride and a ton of personal anger over bosses, all men, who thought equal pay for equal work was a ridiculous concept. I was a woman; therefore I didn't deserve equality. I'd been told that others could treat me as though I were less than needful of justice because, as a child of Max Fisher, I'd had more than my share of wealth. I was Max's daughter; therefore I didn't deserve equality. The men who impressed these views on me had gotten away with it because I didn't know how to fight, or fight back, or win. They had me. I went away meekly. I nursed the idea of revenge, often while nursing a drink.

When I first recognized my anger, and then found a voice to express it, these past injustices whispered to me. But my anger intensified as I became more and more aware of the stigma and shame hurled by society against people with AIDS. This was an anger that did not need to be private. I could express it in public. Rather than self-serving fury, it was infused with a responsibility to defend and protect others like me. It came out in speeches and interviews, when I thought about belittling policies or spoke to national priorities shaped by ignorance and meanness. When my second collection of speeches was published in 1994, it bore the title *I'll Not Go Quietly*, and I meant it. I was venting some public rage. That I vented so pleasantly was mostly a consequence (and in some ways, a benefit) of being a pleaser. I could say very harsh things quite nicely.

Not all who went public with their anger described it in measured tones and respectful comments. Even before I was diagnosed with HIV, I would have been terrified of screenwriter, novelist, and playwright Larry Kramer. He's angry. And no wonder: He'd been in the middle of the plague for a dozen years by the time I was invited to the 1992 convention. That night in Houston, while I was inside the Astrodome speaking nervously about compassion, comfort, and courage, Larry's protestors were outside the arena chanting loudly, hurling insults and condoms at passing motorcades, pointing out to America that they were dying *right there in public.*

Larry cofounded one of the earliest effective AIDS clinics in America, the Gay Men's Health Crisis (GMHC) in New York. He wrote *The Normal Heart*, a shocking, potent play about life and death with AIDS that played off-Broadway in the mid-1980s and made it to Broadway, with rave reviews, almost twenty years later. When Larry created the AIDS Coalition to Unleash Power (ACT UP), he laid the organizational groundwork for AIDS protests in cities and communities across America. He is a large-scale player on the national AIDS stage, and he neither minces words nor pulls punches. The night we met, I was literally trembling at the thought of being near him. The first words I ever spoke to Larry were, "I've been terrified of meeting you."

He smiled, stuck out his hand, and said sincerely, "It is really, really an honor to meet you."

My fear melted, and so did I.

The **truth may not** always work but it is *still* the truth. We do *what is right,* not because it works, but because **IT IS RIGHT.**

Larry came out of the shadows of my own fear and into my heart. He suffers no fear of his own anger, just as he has no fear of love. It's his ability to love deeply that gives poignancy to his writing and power to his plays. In nursing the dying man he loved, his reasoned philosophy was honed into slashing sentences and biting truths. He knew that, up against all the suffering, all the dying, and all the indifference of power and politics, someone needed to scream. He volunteered to go first. And he went to the head of the line—made his scream the first to be heard across Washington, DC, and across every broadcast—because he has no fear of political power, because there is no punishment they could inflict that could approach the gripping horror of the epidemic surrounding him . . . and me.

I've never been a screamer. It's not my way. And it would be unfair to Larry to suggest that he communicates only in one tone or at one volume. He's as overflowing with gentle affection as any human being I've ever known. It was grief that fueled his anger, and courage that helped him express it. What I learned from him is that it's possible to identify your anger, think about it, and then express it—whether in a scream or a speech, using profanity or poetry.

WE WERE TWO YEARS past the speech in Houston when I was invited to speak at a corporate event in New York City. The company's leaders intended to raise both money and awareness to fight AIDS, and they thought having me speak would help.

By the time I mounted their corporate stage in 1994, I knew I was angry, I knew what I was angry about, and I had found a voice in which to express it:

Anger comes when friends die. I was angry when Arthur Ashe died. I was angrier still when Jeffrey Schmalz died. I was angriest of all when I realized how few people really cared that either had come or gone. Even though they were famous, one was black and one was gay—and to be brutally truthful, that had made a difference.

I am angry that we have not valued lives enough to save them, in part because the lives belonged mostly to gay men or poor women, to those who are African or Asian or something other than "we" are. I am angry that someone would think my life is more worthy than theirs because I contracted a virus in marriage, or that someone would think my life is less worthy because I contracted it at all.

I WAS NO LARRY Kramer; what I was saying was not all that radical or even very discomforting. But I was Mary Fisher being honest about anger. Everything I said about anger in these two paragraphs was right on the money. But I had not yet learned the lesson Brian Weiss had been trying to teach me since my diagnosis: that anger and forgiveness (therefore, anger and love) can coexist. As my next few lines demonstrated, in 1994, I still thought love would somehow erase anger:

I was angry that my husband, however unknowingly, played fast and loose with my life and my child's life. I was angry when he told me I needed to be tested and when the results rolled in. But my anger could not repair our relationship; only forgiveness could do that. And when he died in my arms, I had a lot of feelings. Anger was not one of them.

Come forward another four years, and listen to me speak to a group of policy makers and influential women at the White House. It was June 25, 1998, and it was the first time I'd been invited in by the Clinton administration, which had been, in my view, strong on public relations about AIDS but not very helpful on public policy. When in 1997 American AIDS infections reached their highest level ever, the administration's spokesperson offered the good news that the epidemic had "plateaued," sending a shock wave of fury through the surviving AIDS community. I imagine the luncheon planners probably expected something from me that was kinder and gentler than what I delivered:

We want what happens here today to make a difference. We want it to matter. To achieve that, we must go beyond engaging in pleasant conversation to engage some hard realities.

The realities I had in mind included the place on N Street, a few miles from the White House, "where six hundred homeless women will spend their time today: some hopeful, some hopeless, some beyond wondering about hope." And I had some personal realities to add, based on side effects I was enduring from the chemical cocktails that were keeping me alive.

> *We've learned the cost of buying time. Extended days come with a price to be paid in side effects, from "buffalo humps" to "hard, fat bellies" to the depression that nearly turned me suicidal a year ago.*

I took a broad swipe at the administration's use of language to, as I saw it, mute the realities of AIDS:

> *What makes our fear sharpest isn't science, but silence. What was once too frightening to be imagined, a boiling crisis threatening the nation, has been reduced to an "important item on the health care agenda." The epidemic has become "a challenge," unnecessary deaths have become "tragic statistics," and the language of passion has given way to the language of politics.*

And then, amid the elegance of the White House, I let loose my anger:

> *The AIDS crisis is not over. I know, because we have not destroyed the virus. Instead, we have destroyed the urgency. We've allowed the headlines to be all about hope, while the story of dying moved to the obits. We've taken political and economic advantage of good-news announcements. We've let stigma toward gays translate into the dismissal of AIDS. We've watched, with dismay but without panic, as the virus migrated from one minority community to another—now to youth, now to women, now to people of color—each representing a community too small, too disorganized, too passive to create a voting bloc that matters.*

For the first time in such a public setting, I admitted to personal anger that I could no longer contain:

> *To tell you the truth, most days—when I'm not lunching at the White House—I don't care very much. I don't want to be the "AIDS Lady" anymore. I don't care either.*

What I care about is Max, who's ten, and needs to get to the Little League practice; and Zack, who's eight, and sometimes dives into the pool without checking for water. I don't need national declarations and newspaper headlines for the sake of being a hero; I need AIDS to become a crisis again for the sake of two children who are on their way to becoming orphans.

I'm not a researcher, so I'll find no cure. I'm not a White House lawyer, so I'll draft no legislation. I'm a mother who has two children and one very mean virus. And I live expecting that, someday, one of my sons will ask, "So what did you say when you lunched at the White House that time?"

I hope I can say that I warned us all—and their mother first of all—against hypocrisy. If we are called to feed the hungry, but we merely discuss the causes of hunger while the hungry die, we are not yet agents of hope. If we are told, "I am naked," and we respond with a debate on the morality of nakedness, we are agents of hypocrisy, not hope.

In the AIDS epidemic, we cannot hear others say, "We are sick," "We are hopeless," "We are dying," and answer them with, "Yes, yes . . . we talked about you."

If there was any doubt that I'd taken the gloves off, it was answered a few months later—in February 1999—when I was the guest preacher one morning at Washington's towering National Cathedral. More than a dozen years later, I can still hear the audience's gasp when I used language not ordinarily hurled from that famed pulpit:

There was one race in the Garden of Eden, one set of parents, making us one set of brothers and sisters. But after exile from the Garden, our grandparents built a tower at Babel to, as Genesis tells us, "make a name for ourselves."

Race against race, nationality against nationality, gender against gender, party against party—we've continued not only to try to make a name for ourselves but to name others. And we've done it with deadly malice.

We could never have lynched loving black parents of innocent children; but when we named African Americans "niggers," lynching became just a hard night's work. We could never have marched six million human beings into the camps; but when we named my relatives "pigs" and "kikes," we sent them into the ovens believing that we were doing God's will.

Could we drag someone into a field, and beat him, and leave him hanging from a fence to die, if we had learned to call him "Matthew" instead of "fag"? The truth is, we've come stumbling down the corridors of history denying this reality, building our stereotypes, fueling our prejudices, inventing evil names to keep others out of our human family.

The words I was using, the message I was sending, had evolved. I had learned to identify and express anger. It was still mostly dealing with social issues, not interpersonal ones, aimed at the culture of America more than at the soul of Mary. But it was anger, unmasked and fully articulated. What's more, it was mine.

I was angry, and I knew it.

HOUSTON WASN'T MY ONLY experience speaking at a national convention. I also spoke at the 1996 Republican convention in San Diego. Thankfully, no one remembers.

If I'd been naïve enough to expect some kind of RNC '92 redux, that naïveté was soon shaken out of me. Where the 1992 experience was raw and real, made possible at the request of a president, the 1996 version was in the hands of political operatives; it was, from the first step in the process through the final on-stage product, clumsy and rehearsed. At first there was going to be no room for me in the convention program. Then I got an invitation, which I negotiated into a prime-time slot. Then came the news that my time would be shared with woman who was especially good at eviscerating Democrats. I demurred and, for reasons that were never clear but seemed tied to background checks, my speaking partner was dropped from the program.

By the time we arrived in San Diego, I'd gone through three speechwriters, each of whom wanted to put words in my mouth. Then I learned that a new plan had been hatched: I was to mount the podium holding the hand of a photogenic, courageous, HIV-positive child, Hydeia Broadbent, who would then read a poem she'd written. I blanched at the thought. The heartfelt poem of a sick child? People would grieve her AIDS and perhaps mine as well—but this would not be an opportunity to share my anger or rally the troops to action.

When I asked to be allowed to prepare and deliver my own comments introducing and concluding our time on the platform, the convention Powers That Be agreed. So Hydeia and I did the gig. It was artificial and regrettable. My few seconds of advocacy for gay men and African American communities were lost in the din, and my concluding call to "moral courage" was hollow. I went home feeling drained and used. I was also angry.

What was the point? I raged, mostly to myself but also to anyone who would listen. My presence at the '96 convention hadn't done anybody any good. I'd gone to San Diego wanting not to betray myself, my new AIDS community, or the power brokers who'd been part of my life since Mother married Max Fisher. I'd sometimes joke that I was "the only Republican with AIDS," but this was no joke. I feared, deeply, that I might do or say something that would bring hurt to my father, or my family, or President and Mrs. Ford, or others I genuinely loved—but I also feared disappointing those who had welcomed me into the company of the dying: the gay men at the gates, Larry Kramer and his friends—and mine. As it turned out, some of these fears were legitimate concerns. It was not a friendly climate for someone with AIDS who wanted change.

What I really feared wasn't that I would say something wrong but that, in speaking the truth, I would somehow betray those who loved me, my friends old and new. My struggle with the convention organizers was also a struggle over my identity. It raised hard questions about who I was and where I fit in, if anywhere. In a very real sense, San Diego showed me that I was in a battle with myself.

MUCH HAS CHANGED IN the decade and a half that has passed since I fled San Diego. Women finally barged into research projects, thanks to advocates who demanded inclusion on behalf of all who were infected. More knowledge yielded more help, and I survived the years of raising the children, thanks in part to new pharmaceutical aids that at most times evoked fewer and more manageable side effects.

Despite substantial improvements in the drugs, I was feeling less well more often. The peace and quiet I'd hoped to find when we moved to the village north of New York City was elusive. I was, it seems clear in retrospect, searching for contentment within myself. In 2001 we packed up and left a lovely home on the Hudson, moving back to Florida to be nearer to family and to a school that seemed ideal for my sons. By the time the boys were finishing high school, I had discovered Sedona, Arizona.

Sedona is not an angry community. On the contrary, it's deeply calm and spiritual. The red rocks towering over the town are a temple in which Native Americans and Spaniards and now people of every culture have experienced the Divine. Ancient healing ceremonies are viewed as natural, even necessary, in this setting. We moved to Sedona in 2006, and I've never looked back.

My experiment with anger is far from over, though it has been tempered over time by experience, spiritual growth, and probably my own aging. Learning that I harbor anger, and that I can manage it as surely as I can manage other emotions, has been a powerful aid in my life and in my art. It's a spiritual discovery—probably related in some ways to living in Sedona—fostered by a variety of new explorations and adventures.

I was asked a few years ago to join a group of Americans visiting China, and to offer a keynote address to a women's university in an event that would be the centerpiece of our trip. Before and after I was to speak, I was slated to meet national leaders and local advocates to discuss AIDS.

As the group was preparing to leave the United States, China denied my visa. I was refused entrance to the country. The Chinese rationale was painfully simple: The United States wouldn't allow HIV-infected people to come in, so why should China? They had a point, and that left me angry—at both the United States and China. I faced a similar rejection a bit later when I tried to visit Russia. It made me want to scream.

Most days, I do not need to scream. Larry Kramer is, thank God, still capable of orchestrating the screamers. But I now know that when people act without justice, when stigma raises its ugly head or discrimination becomes obvious, a little anger is a good thing. Anger incurred by evil is appropriate, even necessary; anger that transforms how I see other human beings, that makes me see them as evil—this is dangerous territory. I've needed to learn how to love the senator and be angry at the senator's speech.

The only reliable way to distinguish valid anger (or "good anger") from unhealthy anger is to know my own anger and then respond appropriately. It's only taken me a lifetime to do it.

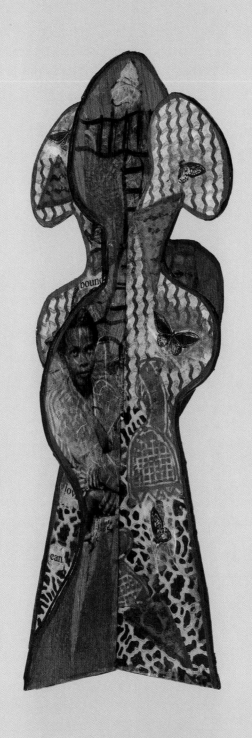

7

Outside Looking In

SIMPLE SOUL

Life is so exhaustingly complicated. Competing priorities, overlapping appointments, torn loyalties, incredible opportunities, financial uncertainties, worn relationships, frightening scenarios . . . and there wasn't enough toothpaste left in the tube this morning. By contrast, my soul is simple. It wants to love and be loved. Amid the chaos and the self-importance, between the urgent and the critical and the impossible—the soul has simple tastes: to love and be loved. Everything else is just frantic decoration.

WE'RE TOLD THAT POLITICS makes for strange bedfellows. So does publishing. When *Reader's Digest* published a condensed version of my 1996 memoir, *My Name Is Mary* (originally released by Scribner), the magazine stationed my copy between that of heroic Captain Scott O'Grady, who had been shot down over Bosnia, and larger-than-life Ben Bradlee, veteran executive editor of the *Washington Post*. O'Grady and Bradley had breath-taking, dramatic stories. My first chapter opened with the limp sentence "All my life I've wanted to be good."

It's probably not even true that I've always wanted to be good. In nice company, I've tried to behave. But I've had my share of adventures and mischief, even if I prefer not to lay them out in gory detail where my children can read about them after I am gone. I've wanted to be a reliable member of my community, whether the community was my school, my workplace, my neighborhood, or even my extended family. I have liked and tried to please those around me. Community expectations matter to me. But being good has its limits.

So does the community in which we find ourselves; it has boundaries that define it and weaknesses that infect it. No community is really universal, and none is perfect.

Community is a tough term to define. Researcher and author Robert Bellah says, in *Habits of the Heart: Individualism and Commitment in American Life*, that it's a word "widely and loosely used by Americans" and that, however we define it, it always represents "an inclusive whole" and "usually explicitly involves a contrast with others."

It seems to me that Bellah is right: Community always has a "we" who are in it and a "they" who are not, an "inclusive whole" only for the folks inside the community circle. We grow up learning who we are, by learning what it means to be part of this "we," part of *our* inclusive whole. According to Bellah,

> we find ourselves not independently of other people and institutions, but through them. We never get to the bottom of ourselves on our own. We discover who we are face-to-face and side by side with others in work, love, and learning. All of our activity goes on in relationships, groups, associations, and communities ordered by institutional structures and interpreted by cultural patterns of meaning . . .

[In a community,] we share certain practices that both define the community and are nurtured by it. Such a community is not quickly formed. It almost always has a history, and so it is also a community of memory.

What is Bellah's point? That a community isn't just a herd in which we skittish antelopes hang out for protection from society's jackals. It's more than a bunch of people, places, and things strewn across our childhood. It's a living environment populated by leaders and followers and scoundrels and saints. It has its own characteristics (think race or language) and develops its own history and character and cooking (think of your grandfather's stories or the smell of your grandmother's kitchen). The concept of community has power, including the profound power to set expectations and measure us against them, thus helping to define who we are and should be by rewarding us for obeying "our" rules and punishing us for violating them.

What I've learned with considerable surprise is that we never outgrow our need to be valued and nurtured by our community. We never graduate. Unless we plan to go into a grueling, hermitlike isolation, some community or other cradles us when we are given a name at the temple or washed at the baptismal font, and it will embrace us when those whose voices we would recognize gather to exaggerate our goodness, to wipe our children's tears, and to bury us.

For some folks, this might be sociology. For me, it's been hard learning. The fact that our communities are deeply involved with our self-definition means I can't put on and take off a community by moving in or out; a community isn't like a change of clothes. Community shapes us as children and sticks with us as adults. Whether we like it or not, community matters. It matters deeply. As we grow older, "our community" may draw elements from various communities in which we've lived, been educated, been challenged and hurt and adored. But whatever our community may be, at any age, it has meaning for our lives. We wake to it every morning, live within it every day, go to bed where we wonder about it during the night.

When word that I had cancer went out through my community, in the town where I live but also on the Internet, and spread through family and friends everywhere, people rallied. Those at a distance sent e-mails and cards and letters. My room filled up with flowers, and my stomach couldn't manage all the chocolates. The outpouring of affection and concern was overwhelming. It was amazing, and it was healing. My community let me know that I mattered.

By contrast, twenty-one years earlier when I'd been diagnosed with AIDS, I very gingerly admitted my diagnosis to a few close friends, my eyes averted and my voice lowered. My room did not fill up with flowers. If anyone sent candy, I don't recall it.

Meanwhile, cancer elicited a thundering *We love you!* from every nook and cranny of my community; AIDS had drawn the terrible silence of a community letting me know that it didn't know what to say.

Silence under such circumstances has the impact of what it is: literally, excommunication. It has been a potent weapon used by religious communities for centuries. If someone explained a new scientific theory that opposed the papal "truth" of that time, the scientist was soon cast out of the fellowship; the faithful were warned to have no communication (or "communion") with him; and silence was to greet him in the marketplace. Excommunication is still effective in tightly drawn, religiously defined communities today. If you've ever had an argument with someone you love, and the argument ended with a slammed door, you don't need to be religious to understand that silence can be very articulate and very effective. In my own case, I got the message loud and clear without the bother of an argument.

I KNEW ABOUT DISCRIMINATION long before I knew about AIDS. I was born in Louisville, Kentucky, and raised in Detroit, Michigan. Both cities have struggled with racial and economic divides. But I'd always been on the safe side of these divides. If the poor suffered injustices at the hands of law-and-order judges, or bigoted employers, or their prejudiced neighbors, I noticed and, as I grew older, I objected. But I wasn't poor—I wasn't the object of these injustices. If black people knew Jim Crow's humiliation with absolute clarity, I knew it merely as something distasteful. I wasn't black.

My first year after being diagnosed as HIV-positive, however, gave me a full taste of intolerance. That year, if reported in some detail, would read like my version of John Howard Griffin's account in *Black Like Me*. Griffin was a white Texan who, in 1959, with a doctor's help, took on the skin color and semblance of a black man. For six weeks he toured the American South by bus and occasionally as a hitchhiker. Griffin went from hearing about segregation to enduring it, from being a member of the oppressor class to being one of the oppressed. His community—what he had believed was his community—no longer wanted him inside the circle. He didn't like it.

I didn't like my AIDS either, but I liked being excluded even less. That the virus brought with it debilitating illness and certain death made it unattractive enough. But what I found especially unnecessary and galling was that AIDS fundamentally changed my relationship with my community. Smiles became raised eyebrows as people wanted to know what I'd done—because surely, whatever it was, I must have violated community standards. I remember exceptions to this unsavory rule, and I remember them by name—women and men who were caring and merciful, whose kindness did not fade when they heard the news. I remember them so clearly *because* they were the exceptions. My dominant experience was that of standing alongside or facing others in my community as they looked the other way. They spoke to one another, not to me—but *about* me.

I knew the voices of my own community—and the silences. As word of my diagnosis went out, messages of disappointment and disapproval came in through the means common in "my" community: Invitations to attend dinner parties dribbled to a stop. The neighbor's children could no longer stay overnight with my sons. The part-time housekeeper didn't dare wash a glass after I'd taken a drink. There were more blatant and obvious affronts, but I didn't need a billboard. The messages were clear.

This discontinuity between my community and me was incredibly disorienting. I vacillated between feeling guilt as if I had done something wrong, and feeling (unadmitted) anger at being made to feel guilty. I wanted to accept my community's approval, even its applause, while deflecting its stigma and discrimination, and I didn't know how to have it both ways. I wasn't yet capable of sorting through the realities of my then community, pushing back against what was wrong and gratefully accepting what was right. So I went looking—literally—for a new community that would match my ideals. Not once but three times, on an exhausting and futile odyssey, I picked up my family and moved on.

Early in this odyssey, in the fall of 1994, I was invited to accept a tribute at the University of Louisville, an annual honor sponsored by the *Louisville Courier-Journal* for "ethical achievement." Louisville was where I'd been born. I had relatives still living there. So I made the following confession to the assembled audience:

> *Being given an award for ethical achievement involves something of a conundrum: I know perfectly well that I'm no hero, and that self-righteousness is not attractive. I have a seven- and a five-year-old at home, both of whom remind me of [my] shortcomings on a daily basis. But having been born in Louisville, and not seeing my relatives very often, it's hard not to find this an attractive way to come home.*

The first community I had ever known had welcomed me back.

My Louisville speech that October afternoon dealt with marketplace ethics—thinking of the marketplace in the historical sense, as a place where men and women sell and shop and everyone shares news and gossip. It was the first time I pointedly acknowledged that forces of stigma and prejudice were not alien to our communities; they were indigenous. We accept, and sometimes we nurture, public opinions that level judgments and punishments against those we judge unworthy. Supported by the almighty power of public opinion, we excommunicate—or worse.

> *Women were dragged from their homes for hangings in Salem, Massachusetts, because public opinion said it was good and right. Slaves were branded and chained and sold at auction, as preachers explained each Sunday that it was God's will. We cannot remember history without seeing marketplace ethics at work.*
>
> *Germany in the 1930s had been rocked by economic and international losses. It was a community hungry for nationalism, for an ethic which said that to be German was to be good—and to be anything less pure was to be evil. It was a short goose-step from this nationalism to the ovens. Marketplace ethics at work.*

I'd been creeping up on these points in earlier speeches but I'd never really applied them to myself, to my self-definition and my self-defined community. But in Louisville I described my appearance at the 1992 convention not in terms of my diagnosis—not in relation to some condition I have—but in terms of who I am. I described my identity as a member of the community.

What shocked America was that a married woman, in her early forties, with two nice children—a Republican, even, with work experience in TV and government—had AIDS. That's all. It wasn't what I said; it's who I represented. At the athletic club in Philadelphia or the bridge club in Kansas City, here was "one of us" instead of "one of them." What made me shocking wasn't my distinctiveness but my commonness. I didn't fit the caricature drawn by American stereotypes. I didn't look like AIDS.

Which is to say: It was less the content of Mary Fisher's speech than the content of America's soul that made my few minutes in Houston newsworthy. It was the stereotype drawn by marketplace ethics that made my appearance surprising.

I had, two years after the convention, begun to understand my own schizoid anxieties when it came to understanding where I belonged and where I could not belong, even if I wanted to. My soul had longed to be among the protestors outside Houston's Astrodome rather than among the Republicans gathered within it. In truth, though, my then chosen community was inside the auditorium. My family members were seated between famous leaders, and the audience contained many of my friends, my power colleagues, my historical

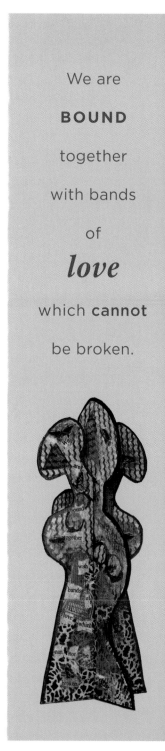

We are

BOUND

together

with bands

of

love

which **cannot**

be broken.

relationships. When I left the stage, I was hugged by TV journalists with whom I'd traveled. I'd slept in the homes of the famous who gathered inside this place; I'd dined with names from the society pages. When I spoke of "public opinion," I was speaking for *our* community—which is to say, theirs but also *mine*.

> *We don't hang Salem women for witchcraft today. But if men are gay, and sick, and dying, and dependent on our charity, they might find hanging a more genteel abuse. We don't trade slaves on the open market today, but we trade in a public opinion [that] reduces whole classes of people to something less than fully human.*
>
> *The voice of public opinion tells us that nice people don't get AIDS. Men must be gay and engaging in unspeakable acts; women must be promiscuous or drug abusers, or both. Children with AIDS are "innocent victims" precisely because adults with AIDS are not. Physicians [have] declined to treat, and morticians [have] declined to embalm, those ravaged by the virus. Where the voice of public opinion sounds like the voice of God, preachers have claimed that God is using AIDS to accomplish His justice. To help God out, some believers have taken time to burn houses of those with AIDS. Here are marketplace ethics at work.*
>
> *The division into "us" and "them" is deadly. It justifies slavery and it fills ovens with Jews. It enabled America to believe it had nothing to fear from AIDS because the majority is heterosexual and we, the majority, were convinced that this was a gay man's disease. Only when the virus began infecting the majority—people like "us" instead of "them"—did our conscience awaken.*

I had only just begun to understand who I was in the context of community, any community. If I was ambivalent—wanting in and out at the same time—so, it seemed, was my community. It didn't know what to do with me either. The dominant wish was, I think, to make an exception for me and a few others. As I remembered in Louisville, "Legislation is named not for one of the hundreds of thousands of gay men who have died, but for Ryan White, a charming, young, and heterosexual teenager. These are acceptable: Arthur Ashe, Elizabeth Glaser, Magic Johnson . . . and Mary Fisher." These people could belong to our community. These few could be given a place—a place carefully segregated and broadly recognized.

"His mother has AIDS, you know," would be said of my son, who would move to that place with me. What the mother wanted to say, because she loved her child and didn't understand people with AIDS, was "You should be nice to Max, but don't go to his house or share his lunch." Fear dominated: my fear of rejection and their fear of an illness they didn't understand.

To draw on the biblical distinction, those of us who had AIDS plus name recognition and money were *in* the community but not *of* it. And God help the vast majority of those with AIDS and no fame—those who lacked Magic's smile or Arthur's genius, those who were not among the "innocents."

AFTER HOUSTON, WHEN I began speaking extensively, I needed some way to describe people with AIDS besides "people with AIDS." I detested the word *victim* because it signaled passivity and pathos. Where there are victims, there is pity. Yuck. I couldn't call us all "patients"; that worked in the doctor's office but not in the legislative assembly or the Methodist church. I finally settled on "a company of pilgrims." The word *pilgrim* signaled innocence, the search for something pure and holy, and I applied it to everyone on the road to AIDS— no matter who they were or how the virus had found them. By saying everyone HIV-positive was "on the road to AIDS," I could pick up and use the imposition of two terms for one illness: *HIV-positive* so long as your T-cell count was over 200, *AIDS* as soon as it was below that demarcation. The term *pilgrim* was just religious enough to take a swipe at language used by religious bigots. And it had the virtue of suggesting that we were going somewhere. Besides, being a pilgrim was more flattering than being a fallen woman. So I could speak of us as "a company of pilgrims marching inevitably to our deaths."

Who might actually be included among the pilgrims, I left a little vague. Organizations such as Larry Kramer's ACT UP were an expression of a raging, dying gay community. But this community, like all, had reasonable boundaries: What about those of us with AIDS who are not gay? And would that community also include not only people with AIDS but their caregivers, physicians, and researchers? Perhaps policy makers and journalists and health care bureaucrats belong to this community too? But having some interest in a topic—even when that topic is an illness that represents your life work—doesn't define you; it isn't a part of who you are. Ultimately, I learned (as did others) that it was no easier to define an AIDS community than, say, an arthritis community. A disease does not a community make.

The one moment in which I thought that America might actually have an AIDS community of substance and meaning, of the kind described by Robert Bellah, came in the summer of 1996. The NAMES Project Foundation's Memorial Quilt had been brought to Washington, DC. It was a presidential election year and the media was especially prolific. The quilt had grown so large that this display, spread across the grass-and-concrete stretch between the Washington Monument and the Lincoln Memorial, was to be its last as a single unit.

The final evening of the event began with a candlelight procession starting from the steps of the Capitol and winding alongside the quilt all the way to the Lincoln Memorial, where a concluding program would bring closure to the display. I was among the scheduled program speakers, so I was near the front of the march with the boys. I didn't have enough hands to hold on to Max, Zack, and three dripping candles—it was a real balancing act. I'd begun the day emotionally exhausted and physically aching, and the summer heat had worn me down. But the evening was cool and perfect. My tiredness faded as we exchanged hugs with laughing friends. Somewhere behind us a male chorus was singing *We Shall Overcome* and then *Blowin' in the Wind*. I remember tears when, just as I was looking across the thousands of panels of the quilt, those incredible a cappella voices took up the sweet harmony of *Amazing Grace*. We all grew silent, knowing with a terrible certainty that we were both marchers and mourners.

As the hymn's melody floated from behind us, I heard a shout up ahead. I thought someone had fainted or an accident had happened. But as we kept walking, I realized the noise was coming from protestors standing on the sidewalk, waving signs, pointing Bibles and hurling insults at the passing marchers. These were "Christians" who'd driven a thousand miles from, I think, some Kansas church to practice their zealotry in language I did not want my children to hear. I thought about running, then I considered covering their ears, but already I was out of hands. There was no place to go but forward, nothing to do but listen. I let the candles go out, held one of Max's hands and one of Zack's, and we marched forward through screams of "Die! Die! Die!" and "God hates fags!" and "God, God, God gave you AIDS, AIDS, AIDS!"

Journalists who covered the event spoke mostly of the AIDS "movement," maybe because we evoked memories of civil rights marchers, and the fight for civil rights in this nation was known as a "movement." But among my moments on the road to AIDS, this was the one in which I felt as though the AIDS *community* was most real. We were an inclusive whole, those of us holding hands and candles and children. Our reality explicitly contrasted with others represented by the screaming "Christians" who'd slithered across the map to assault us. Having a community of marchers meant that I was one of many, that the boys and I were commoners, just three of the gang of thousands. The virus had become our family's price of admission, not a curse of exclusion. This one evening, I knew who I was and who we were, because the marchers constituted a community. It was a glorious moment amid a horrendous plague set alongside a memorial to grief.

The ideal of an AIDS community died hard for me. Seven years after that evening in Washington, a dozen years after my diagnosis, I had given up my idealistic notion—or at least I said I had. At the 2003 speech in Denver where I entertained both the audience and a heart attack, I told the National Association of People with AIDS (NAPWA) that, whatever else we were, we were not a community.

Perhaps the hardest recognition for me, or for us, is that we call ourselves "a community" but we have not yet really become one. AIDS has not united groups otherwise divided by economics and race and language. We are separated by drugs some of us can afford and swallow with guilt while others are denied access. We are divided by failure to engage communities where the virus is most virulent: communities of color, of poverty, of immigrants, of youth. We can raise our glasses in this splendid place, saluting ourselves, but there are those in hospices who do not know NAPWA and those in flophouses for whom even a hospice is out of reach.

If once there had been an AIDS "movement," by 2003 it had largely dissolved. It had withered under the relentless tortures of illness, discrimination, and hopelessness. Voices of power and grace were momentarily raised, then stilled by death. By the mid-1990s most of the women and men who represented AIDS in America had wasted into silence. Some uninfected professional leaders moved on to other causes, other issues, other career positions. Hollywood starlets found new fads. The red ribbon was eclipsed by a trendier campaign, a different-colored ribbon. ARV drugs arrived, raising the possibility that death sentences could be stalled if not commuted, and promoting the myth that AIDS had been "cured" (thus setting off new rounds of infections among vulnerable populations). Meanwhile, someone diagnosed with AIDS today has her treatment largely and ineffectively "mainstreamed" in America's health care system. Urban areas where HIV figures are through the roof may still have an "AIDS clinic," but most institutions founded by that name have become part of the broader systems of care. For all these reasons and more, whatever budding community we'd cobbled together has largely unraveled.

Of the AIDS organizations planted twenty years ago, the Elizabeth Glaser Pediatric AIDS Foundation and the American Foundation for AIDS Research (amfAR) remain the most active. Both are important and have done much good. Elizabeth's foundation, by virtue of her passion for women and children, has never been closely identified with gay men or most shunned groups. amfAR has also stayed out of the fray over civil rights and human justice, benefiting from Elizabeth Taylor's endless commitment while staying focused on science and medicine. But if, even today, a crossword puzzle were to say *gay men's illness*, Americans would write in *AIDS*. If the clue said *women's illness*, most Americans would answer *breast cancer*. Gay men get the blood-red scarlet letter of AIDS; women get the sweet, lovable pink of roses and Cadillacs.

Still . . .

Not long ago I was in Minnesota working on an art project when I bumped into some people attending a conference. A lobby poster told me they had convened to discuss AIDS. They were health care workers, policy makers, counselors, people with AIDS, chaplains, family members, and caregivers who'd lost loved ones. They'd come together to work on legal rights, social justice, new drugs, old challenges, and the environment surrounding AIDS in Minnesota. I was thrilled to meet them and honored when a few remembered me. And I thought to myself when we left them that night, *Maybe there is an AIDS community after all. Maybe it's just not as visible or noisy as we once were.* Maybe it doesn't need to be.

IF I WANTED, TWENTY years ago, to help surround myself with an AIDS community, perhaps I should have tried to build it out of women. Instead of finding my identity and home in the American gay community—whose welcome and support have nonetheless been incredibly important to me—maybe I should have looked to develop a community of women with AIDS.

In some respects, Dawn Averitt Bridge has led the way toward such a community with her Women's Research Initiative, begun in 2003. A tireless advocate and skilled negotiator, she's gathered women with AIDS and those who care about them in projects that have led to change. No one has done more than Dawn to get women and women's issues as priorities in research projects. That women are still underrepresented in such research is unfortunate, but that we are represented at all is largely owing to the efforts of Dawn and her colleagues.

I did not know, in 1992, how to find other women with AIDS. There was no Internet—at least not as we have it today. Most AIDS institutions were dominated by men and tied in some way to gay support systems without which they would have died. But when I began to give speeches, I began to find the women. They were at Rikers Island and Stand Up Harlem and the First AME Church of Los Angeles. They were in the clinics and neighborhood centers in Chicago and Kansas City, Phoenix and Syracuse. I found them hiding their infections in plain sight, among the Baptist and Congregational and Methodist and Catholic and Jewish congregations where I was allowed to speak. They were on college campuses and in high school assemblies. They were everywhere I went, and they were terrified.

Among the many things that frightened them was a legal system that criminalized women. A few prosecutors, whether out of ignorance or ambition (or both), saw to it that several HIV-positive women had their children removed from them, because having AIDS surely proved these women were undesirable, dangerous mothers. A few well-placed headlines about such stories taught American women the obvious lesson: *Don't tell. Don't ever, ever tell.*

Silence and fear have been the two chief characteristics shared by American women with AIDS. It was so at the beginning and it's still so now. And the consequence of silence and fear is death. If you're a woman in an immigrant community where you are not taught—or not allowed—to speak English, shop, drive, or speak to strangers, and if your partner has brought home AIDS, you are going to die. The power of that community's standards will overwhelm the power of fear, even fear of dying.

If you are a woman in an abusive relationship, or a girl held in slavery by means of addiction and violence, or a coed cheerleader at a football powerhouse—if you fit any of these categories, and you've been infected with HIV, you're in deep trouble. It is unlikely that you will find the help you need as early as you need it. Your best hope is that your AIDS will progress to the point where symptoms make you too ill to avoid real medical care. At that point, you will become useless to your abuser, your partner, your owner, or your football team; they'll let you go. If you somehow find your way into the health care system, you may yet live.

What fear is not generated by personal intimidation can be created by social norms. A woman who says "I want an AIDS test" is, by virtue of the request, judged guilty of playing with danger: dangerous sex, dangerous drugs, or dangerous people—maybe all three. All hope for self-image and acceptance is challenged by the fear of being found out. For every woman who tests or considers testing for AIDS, lurking in the shadows is the fear of losing her adult relationships, losing her job, and (for mothers) losing her children.

If these fears seem exaggerated, it's not because I'm exaggerating them. Come with me to any sizable audience with women present. After I speak, they want to meet privately. Sometimes those who've been diagnosed HIV-positive know each other and find a room in the basement where I'm led to hear their stories. Often they have, until this moment, never met another woman with AIDS. Their fear has isolated them. Knowledge frees us. So after I've spoken, they use a hug as a means to get close and whisper in my ear, "I have AIDS too, but nobody knows. . . ." Except, of course, now somebody does know: me. It's a beginning.

Studies have recently suggested that communication bonds between women hold together entire civilizations and cultures, not only in communities of chimpanzees and elephants but also in the human world. Women's Circles, some of them now global and viral, feed on and foster sisterhood. We women bond in ways men cannot bond, just as we conceive children in ways they cannot. It is neither righteous nor wrong; it is merely the reality. And if I add my belief to this reality, it leaves me with the conviction that women can access a spiritual connection that's uniquely feminine and uniquely powerful.

As a quilter myself and a woman with AIDS, I've always loved the irony that the American memorial for AIDS, the "gay men's illness," is a quilt. Those who know the history of quilting know that it is a history of storytelling. A quilt carries history in the stories that accompany the used fabrics: Uncle John's shirt gave the quilt its navy blue. Grandma Shannon's nightgown offered edging. When, a century and more ago, women gathered in quilting bees, it was not only to share pieces of cloth or to borrow a sharper needle. A quilting bee was the place where a woman found safe companionship and comfort, where lessons of economics and homemaking and sexuality and marriage could all be taught by elder sisters who'd accumulated years of wisdom. Over the clacking of knitting needles and the sound of ripping cloth, women shared stories of men's foibles and sometimes bawdy humor that would have scandalized the menfolk.

When I visualize the quilting bee, I can imagine a community of American women with AIDS, but the reality is that I have not found it, nor would I know how to create it. Fear is too dominant, and silence is too effective. I would not know how to recruit those who most need the knowledge, companionship, and skills such a community could offer. But I would recognize such a community here in the United States if I ever experienced it. I know, because I have experienced it—just not in my own country.

In the late 1990s I was invited to join a White House–sanctioned delegation visiting a half dozen African nations, ostensibly to find out what progress they were or were not making in the fight against AIDS. At each stop, the American contingent, mostly white, would line one side of a table in a government office; the African representatives, mostly black, would line the other. It was suggested that, as the Africans dutifully reported on their efforts, we should nod and take notes, not interrupt, ask what we could do to help, hear responses, say "Thank you," and leave. And that would be it.

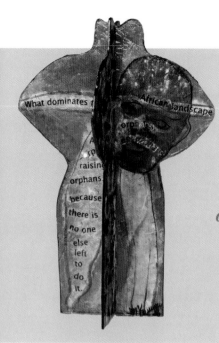

What DOMINATES

the *African* landscape

is acres of orphans:

orphans raising orphans,

because there is

no one else left to do it.

I did this once, and then I protested. I explained to our delegation leader that I was sincerely appreciative of what was being said and done, but strange as it may seem, my heart wasn't on our side of the table. I was obviously white and American, but every time a black African woman with AIDS spoke for her nation, I was with her. I adored the senator who traveled with us, and I was truly grateful for the protocol that had been negotiated in advance to make this endeavor work. But it wasn't working for me. I was one of "them," not one of "us."

At our next stop, I was permitted to speak briefly. I don't recall just what I said, but it wasn't much more than "I, too, am a woman with AIDS." Some of our African hosts were shocked because they'd never before met a white woman with AIDS; they may not have truly believed it was possible—that I was possible. The response in the first nation where I spoke up, and in each thereafter, was a collective silence while all the air went out of the room, then an explosion of murmuring, smiles, and hugs. African women had never heard a stranger make so personal a confession as "I have AIDS." When they realized I'd told the truth, their reaction was the same as mine: We belonged on the same side of the table.

Since that trip, I've returned to Africa repeatedly. Once there, I am—at last—part of a community of women with AIDS. The racial and national divides between us are short and easily spanned by what we share: a virus that wants to kill us. We are women together, daughters and sisters together, mothers together. We laugh, we sing, we dance, we cry, we hug, we whisper, we promise. This isn't all easy, and some of the issues we face are grotesquely hard. But all the challenges and differences are diminished by the community that holds us, binds us, defines us, and frees us.

The first time I came home from Africa, I was depressed. I didn't want to be home. I wanted to go back to Zambia or Rwanda, to one of the places where I'd been one of the women with AIDS. I tried to explain this to a friend and, while I know she loves me, it made no sense to her. She was baffled. Maybe I was too. It's taken more than a decade to realize that the highs of being in Africa and the low points in the United States are merely the flip sides of the coin named *community*.

MY LONGING TO FIND a place where I belong isn't a result of AIDS. It's a consequence of being human. I had the longing as a child in Detroit, as a young adult in Israel, as a woman in Paris and New York City and elsewhere. It may have escalated when I felt the sting of stigma and heard the messages of exclusion, all owing to my AIDS. But AIDS did not cause the longing. We all want someplace to belong. We all find ourselves in the context of others, because there's no other way to be born, live, and die. We draw our sense of right and wrong from our communities, our understandings of beauty, shame, humor, heroism, and ambition. Our communities have histories and memories, and we want to find ourselves within those memories and to earn a place of honor in those histories. It's natural.

It may also be natural for Americans of my generation to develop an idealized, small-town concept of community: Norman Rockwell is sketching at the corner drugstore, the town cop is helping a child find her way home, yards have white picket fences, and bikes are casually strewn around the baseball diamond where kids are playing softball.

When I moved with the children to a small town north of New York City, that's probably what I was looking for. Had you called me on it, I'd have denied it with a quick "I know better than that." I knew Ozzie and Harriet had moved on and Beaver wasn't living in our town. But that small-town ideal was still what I longed for and was hoping to find—if not in the perfect ideal, then close enough to merit being called "community."

What I now know is that I can live without having every ideal fulfilled. After all, small towns come with their own challenges. There's no anonymity in a small town, even where it would be appropriate. Gossip is, for better or worse, a trusted communication network. Local historians have a better memory for who got pregnant during high school than for who was valedictorian. Sometimes we're neither forgiving nor accepting. We are human, and our community reflects our human nature.

Sedona, where I now live, is good. It's by far the most accepting community in which I've tried to plant my roots, and I draw a straight line between Sedona's historical role as a spiritual center and its welcoming-with-open-arms community today. Looking around this community, I realize that I'm becoming one of the elder sisters. It irritates me, and it delights me, and it even amuses me. I didn't expect to be this old. Now that I am, I need, in my own small ways, to help set the cultural tone of this community. I can't merely rail against the unfairness of judgmentalism or whine about some other community's warped standards. I need to demonstrate a better way. Else I'm not an advocate so much as a hypocrite.

One of my sculptures bears these words: "Community is a fragile creature and we are called to nurture it, to help it grow vigorously and grow strong. I guess I need to listen to myself."

And if I find myself reading, say, the *New York Times*, hoping for a good review of my art or my book or my life, I might also go back to reread my blistering speech at the University of Louisville:

Mark Twain may be right. He once described how gossip is elevated to the level of gospel by giving it a new label: "Its name is Public Opinion," he wrote. "It is held in reverence. It settles everything. Some think it is the voice of God."

Where my community is swayed most by Public Opinion, my true value won't be measured by a donation to the community theater or a speech for the community foundation. The true measure of my value is tested by this simple standard: Have I in some way enabled my community to be more generous, more accepting, more decent, and more just?

If so, I have come to town as a messenger of compassion. If not, I'm just the lady who wears the red ribbon, one more name on the tax rolls.

8

Is There a Leader in the House?

Some from our class went on to become rich and powerful. He, brilliant, stuck to his plan: He became a teacher of English. When students write papers for him, he not only reads them, he answers them. He teases teenagers into celebrating Tolstoy's courage and Twain's wit, and he leads the celebration. His letters— oh, to receive one of his letters! Humbly, gently, he writes to raise my spirits. He convinces me that life matters. He says I matter. Could there be a more precious soul than his?

I NEVER SET OUT to become a leader. Looking back, and looking around, it appears I've successfully avoided becoming one. I'm an artist, and it has taken me decades to become comfortable with just that description. But I am not, do not want to be, have never claimed to be, and will not be found guilty of being a leader.

Management guru Peter Drucker cut through all sorts of refined definitions to give this one: A leader is someone who has followers. That seems right to me. We have mountains of people who bray about their credentials as leaders, but if no one is following them, they're not leading; they're just making noise.

I treasure two examples of leaders from the past, and they aren't exactly a natural couple: Susan Brownell Anthony and Moses. Moses was trailed by the Israelites for forty years, out of slavery in Egypt but not quite into the Promised Land. Susan B. Anthony wrote, spoke, protested, was threatened with violence and jail, and never lived to see women step into the voting booth. Moses speaks to the Jewish part of me; Susan B. Anthony speaks to the woman in me. Both fascinate me because they claimed they were unworthy, they struggled, they were slandered, and they died before their prize was won. Moses didn't get into the Promised Land he'd sought, but his followers did. Ms. Anthony was dead fourteen years when her followers won the Nineteenth Amendment and stormed the polls. And the fact that neither saw the goal achieved is part of why I like them so much. This demonstrates that leadership isn't really about leaders; it's about followers.

I knew early in this journey that I was destined to be a follower. I didn't choose to enter the American struggle with AIDS; I was drafted by a virus. Anyone who would want to lionize me must remember that I did not get here by courageous choice: I was dragged in, struggling and wailing. I had zero interest in being the American AIDS princess and no desire to be a leader of an American AIDS community. Most leaders can give a speech, but giving a speech does not make one a leader any more than, as Billy Sunday liked to say, "standing in the garage makes you a car." I was running from fear when I spoke in Houston, not running for office. I've spent most of my years on the road to AIDS looking for someone to follow.

A decade and a half after my HIV diagnosis, while giving a keynote speech to a group of philanthropic executives and donors, I recalled my hope of finding leadership:

Early on, we who were dying thought AIDS would find persuasive voices and charismatic leaders, that what Martin Luther King brought to the American civil rights movement, some hero would bring to our movement.

I had reflected on my experiences in Africa and in hundreds of American communities, remembering where the AIDS movement had been and where the virus was now, worldwide. Our "Dr. King" had never arrived. We were followers without a leader.

Hope has not triumphed, stigma has not been erased, and the dying has been as stubborn as the virus itself. What the American AIDS community has always lacked is leadership. Those with AIDS learned early that dead leaders are ineffective leaders.

Changing cultures is hard and slow. Africa is still poor. Asia is still in denial. America has pursued other wars. Satellites and the Internet have taught us to think globally, but millions of dusty orphans wandering the sub-Saharan [region] move most policy makers to nothing more than a sigh. Young people think AIDS has been cured. Communities of color, of women, of immigrants, of drug users, of trafficked sex workers, of the rural poor, and of urban ghettoes—these have something in common: They lack prestige, they lack power, and therefore they lack hope. They also lack leadership. What they do not lack is AIDS.

I spoke of the power that flowed from Dr. King's rich baritone—power that our movement lacked—and lamented "facing the greatest health crisis in human history, knowing it comes with no identifiable global movement and without a single, morally persuasive spokesperson." Lack of powerful leadership left those fighting both stigma and the virus without a source of power, rage, hope, and direction—all things King had given to the American civil rights movement.

The challenges are compounded by geography. In the West, vertical transmission from mothers to infants is virtually eradicated; in Africa and the East, vertical transmission remains a huge challenge. [Plus,] the epidemic traces trucking routes in one nation and drug routes in another—trafficking in this country and sexual taboos in that. In the West, governments are increasingly unable or unwilling to pay for the treatment of those who previously [would have] died but now stay alive. In Africa and Asia, dying remains relentless, devastating work forces, economies, families, and nations—[while] governments, unable to stop the epidemic with public policy, adopt a stance of public denial. Skyrocketing infection rates are not good for political careers or tourism.

We are in a peculiar spot. We have enough science to find and treat AIDS. We have the medical knowledge we need to keep people alive. Nonetheless, tens of millions of people are dying, creating something on the magnitude of fifteen million orphans—numbers that climb by the hour. How is this possible when we have enough science to stop it?

It is possible because communities and nations require leaders. Without leadership, vision is impossible. Without leadership, individuals and families pursue only their own missions, their own welfare, their own interests . . .

There are individuals who have, in specific times and ways, made great contributions to those of us with AIDS. Some were scientists, some caregivers, some politicians and policy makers, some artists and activists. In a real sense, each led the way to new knowledge and new hope. But looking across the landscape of AIDS in the United States and globally, no living figure stands tall enough to be, say, the Desmond Tutu or Cesar Chavez—or the Moses or Susan B. Anthony—of AIDS.

FIVE AMERICAN PRESIDENTS HAVE presided over the American AIDS epidemic. The first, President Reagan, stayed so far from the issue that he was not heard to utter the word *AIDS* in public until his seventh year in office. And then only once.

Since President Reagan, the Oval Office has been occupied by two Bushes, a Clinton, and an Obama. Those who have left office show a character that wasn't always apparent when they lived at 1600 Pennsylvania Avenue. Once they were freed of the presidency, both presidents Bush and their wives spoke pointedly and compassionately on the challenges of AIDS in the United States and elsewhere. President Clinton has taken strong and positive stands on the issue since he left office in 2001. But judged only on their time in the Oval Office, the record of presidential leadership for Americans with AIDS is unremarkable.

In terms of the *American* AIDS epidemic, the Clinton administration was viewed as the most friendly but didn't get great grades for actual support. It was strong on public relations and wanted the gay vote. But if President Clinton understood our pain, he didn't do much to relieve it— nor have the administrations of President Bush the first, President Bush the second, or (as I write) President Obama.

In terms of the *global* AIDS epidemic, the second President Bush— George W.—is remembered with deep respect for a program known mostly by its acronym, PEPFAR: the President's Emergency Plan for AIDS Relief. Beginning early in his first term, this President Bush presided over the largest amount of funding any single nation had ever invested against any single disease. Administration insiders have sometimes assigned credit for the program to the then secretary of state Colin Powell and to the president's persuasive wife, Laura. Since leaving office, President Bush also has created an institute to focus attention and resources on AIDS in the United States and globally. But PEPFAR stands above all other efforts over the thirty-year period beginning in 1981. If President George W. Bush is remembered more gratefully in Nigeria and Rwanda than in New York and Raleigh, PEPFAR is the reason. It has made a tremendous difference to countless people.

Years earlier, midway through the first President Bush's term, Congress and the president jointly named a National Commission on AIDS. It was the first high-ranking governmental recognition that an epidemic was under way. The commission's stated purpose was to coordinate policies and promote strategies to more effectively combat AIDS. Its understood purpose was to serve as a political shock absorber between a bewildered political apparatus and a raging gay community.

During the 1992 presidential campaign, Magic Johnson, whom President Bush had earlier named to the commission, resigned. His resignation made a few headlines and created one vacancy. My appointment as his replacement garnered some media attention but was not a great surprise since it came less than two months after the Republican National

Convention. AIDS was a hot media topic, and the race for the White House was close, so when the commission met, it drew plenty of attention.

I accepted the president's appointment to the commission because I had enormous respect for the presidency, respect that had been elevated by my time serving President Ford. And I felt as though I owed one to President Bush: Had he not given his personal thumbs-up, I'd never have received a prime-time spot at the 1992 convention. But there were also personal factors. I genuinely believed that, as a person with AIDS on the commission, I might be able to make a difference. I thought my voice could matter. This made me idealistic at the very least, and probably naïve. What I expected of members of Congress and a sitting president, and of my ability to reach and persuade any of them, was out of touch with reality as I now know it.

But on this one score I may have been right: I was certain that the AIDS community needed leadership from some quarter and that without it, we were doomed.

Speaking at a Presidents' Day luncheon in New York City in 1993, after the election had been settled in favor of President Clinton, I observed that a "BBC journalist filing reports from the Iowa primary . . . opened one story with this line, 'It's a bloody strange process that gets Americans their presidents.'" After affirming that sentiment, I went on:

A herd of candidates thunders into our living rooms, each member wanting to prove that he is more worthy than any other to lead where we would follow. Each claims a unique call to mount the "bully pulpit" that arises from the Oval Office. And we listen whether we like it or not, because—deep down—the truth is, we want to believe it. Beyond the campaigns made noisy with the rhetoric of promises, what we are looking for, longing for, is a leader we can champion.

The hunger in this nation for leadership is palpable. Maybe it's the kind of hunger that arose from German poverty in the 1930s to set the stage for the Little Fuhrer. The national appetite for one hero, one person of dignity and courage, is undeniable . . .

And if the nation is hungry for leadership, there is no community within America that cries out for leadership more adamantly or with more reason than the AIDS community—the band of one or two million pilgrims who find themselves marching the road to AIDS.

Amid cameras and shouted questions, I had taken my seat on the National Commission on AIDS, ready to find a leader. Eight months later—in June 1993—the Clinton administration effectively disbanded the National Commission on AIDS by not extending its term. Two other advisory bodies were eventually created, and I served on one of them. But nothing was ever again given the power or drama of that first commission, in part because it was first and in part because of the political tensions and rage surrounding AIDS during those times.

The original National Commission on AIDS might have succeeded in raising some national consciousness and, among those with AIDS, a bit of hope. But it never became a dynamic force for change. It gave the media an institution to monitor, and it provided a buffer of sorts between those with power and those with AIDS. Its members were well-intended, and its organizers were earnest. But our achievements were, in a word, lame. The commission was not a collective leader, and no one member's voice gained staying power.

My tenure on the commission coincided with what was to be the heaviest speaking schedule of my life. In addition to appearances I'd approved earlier, I took on events Arthur Ashe was too ill to attend, adding his commitments to my own. I'd just returned from Arthur's funeral, in fact, when it became clear that Brian's AIDS had moved to end-stage. All of it—the illnesses and death, my sickness and fear, the children, crowds, the commission, speeches, the media—all of it was taking a toll. I didn't miss a single event, drop any dates, or renege on any promises. But I would go to bed too drained to sleep and wake up too tired to smile. I loved my children, but I was struggling to keep up with them.

Brian's calls became unpredictable as fevers burned and blinding headaches kept him bedridden. When Brian died, I tried to comfort Max and Zack even as I realized this was what my own future would be like. Amid this blur of events, I took a call from Dr. June Osborn, chair of the National Commission, who said she'd scheduled a Washington, DC, news conference to mark the commission's demise. Under the circumstances, she said, "Don't feel you need to come." But if I was "up to it," she added, she'd be grateful if I'd speak to the media.

I flew from Brian's funeral to the commission's news conference. Had I been fresh and perky, perhaps my part would have gone more smoothly.

As it was, I could barely read my prepared comments and, when I did, I only stammered through them:

> *The commission is packing up and going home. And so am I. But I will not go passively or quietly . . . I am going to ask for leadership today, and again tomorrow, and I am going to raise my voice each time I ask, until those who have asked for confidence have earned it—by leading.*
>
> *Let me be clear: It is not the AIDS community itself that is desperate for leadership; it's the nation at large. Those who imagine that this is someone else's problem, someone else's disease—these are people who need leaders, or they will surely die. The senator who compares HIV-positive immigrants with infected fruit, the preacher who regards the virus as God's good idea—these justify our call to leadership.*
>
> *Most of all, the nation needs moral leadership. Without it, we will perish; with it, there is hope. Morally, it is no more possible to think of this as a crisis for the infected than it is to think of slavery as an African American problem, the Holocaust as a Jewish program, or abuse as a child's problem. When this message finds a leader to deliver it, convincingly, we will begin to understand as a nation that this is* our *crisis. . . .*
>
> *I need to go home and answer hard questions from two children. But* someone *needs to lead. . . .*

Maybe my call for leadership was little more than an emotional appeal for *someone* to do *something*. I was exhausted, infected, and emotionally raw. I'd gone from Arthur's funeral to Brian's bedside, and then from Brian's funeral to the closing of the commission. I now knew what tens of thousands of gay men had experienced when they held lovers as they died, each of them seeing what their own deaths would be like just a little ways down the road. And the commission's demise said to me, rightly or wrongly, that Washington's power structure did not care.

And, although I might have denied it at the time, I was angry. I was angry that this president had promised change but now appeared to be more interested in good press than good policy. I was angry that we on the commission were being dismissed, sent home as if we did not matter. I was angry that Arthur was dead, and Brian was dead, and I was dying.

I was angry that there was nowhere to turn and no leader to inspire us. I was angry at the very thought that my crusade to persuade those in power was little more than Mary Fisher tilting at Washington's windmills.

MONTHS TURNED TO YEARS, and no charismatic leader swept in to save us. Death rates had skyrocketed in 1993 as infections from the early and mid 1980s took their inevitable toll. The dying increased in '94 and again in '95, even as rumors of a new "drug cocktail" began to surface. Most people with AIDS were attending funerals where, after the service, everyone discussed their fear of being led down the AZT path to disappointment. When drug companies whispered "Hope" to approximately a million people, we stayed mostly hopeless.

The cocktail, which we now know as ARVs, was coming on the scene as I was moving into near-continuous bouts of illness. I and a few others created a nonprofit organization, the Family AIDS Network, to link families impacted with AIDS to one another and to local resources. Representative Steve Gunderson retired from his congressional seat representing western Wisconsin and took on the work of organizing and leading our network. For a while, expecting that I would soon get ill and die, I imagined that the network would carry on my mission when I was gone.

But the earliest of the new ARV drug regimens was keeping me alive, even if it also kept me sick. I lived on the edge of depression, sometimes just above it and sometimes below it, but I didn't know if it was a side effect of drugs or a side effect of dying. When the drugs had been researched, no women had been involved as subjects; the obvious result was that side effects in women were totally unknown. As my physical and emotional health slid out from under me, so did my capacity to support the Network with media and public appearances, and especially with keynote speaking engagements. I remember saying on more than one occasion in the late 1990s, "I can't do it anymore." We dissolved the Network in 2000 at Steve's urging, and to my relief, and we moved our resources to the Clinical AIDS Research and Education (CARE) Fund at the University of Alabama at Birmingham. The CARE Fund did not need me to be healthy or to lead, and it continues to serve the AIDS community well today.

If the Family AIDS Network was my attempt at providing leadership, it also failed. The work of the network was admirable, and I look back without regret. But it did not, and I could not, rally an AIDS community into existence. On a few issues and a few occasions, we offered a leadership voice. Overall, we did not provide leadership.

It's hard not to play a bit of the *What if . . . ?* game—not to wonder whether leadership would have arisen from the gay community had most of its brilliant leadership not been infected. Larry Kramer survived, as did a few other strong voices, but they were the exceptions who stayed afloat as the cruiser sank. "Much of the gay community's AIDS leadership did not survive," I remembered with a New York City audience in 2011, leaving us all to speculate about what might have happened had AIDS not been lethal.

Demographics and time worked against them. Those who lived struggled with their own health and, when they looked around, saw no one left to lead. The epidemic that had so visibly attached itself to the gay community migrated, infection by infection, down the path of viral epidemics to the poor, the immigrant, the unlucky lover. Next to the AIDS community, Occupy Wall Street looks well-organized. In the American mind, AIDS went home to Africa; in the American reality, AIDS went underground. Underground, it's beyond the sight of policy makers, editors, and politicians, happily watching clinics lose funding and staff. Underground, it feeds on the vulnerable, including the next generation of gay youth . . .

The gay community does not need to die again for the AIDS community to be revived. What we need is leadership—leadership willing to reach underground to the frightened and the dying, leadership capable of calling those who have grown weary to come and walk with us again.

Even now, I've not entirely forsaken the hope that some Moses will be hiding in the bulrushes, or some Susan B. Anthony will come out of the crowd. An articulate, committed leader could change the course of the AIDS epidemic in America and around the globe. This person would hold the bigots accountable for their hypocrisy and hate, would lift the spirits of the sick and dying, would speak truth to those in power. This leader would lead, and we would follow. It could happen. And if it does, those who've taken their AIDS underground will reappear. Men too tired to care will get a second breath. Women who live in silent, dying terror will find their voices. Hope will rise on the wings of inspiration.

For my part, I'll give speeches, write the occasional book, and continue to create art. I'll do my best to tell the truth. And part of the truth is my longing for that absent leader.

Every four years, when the season of campaigns and slogans returns, I'm reminded of George Orwell's advice regarding leaders. "High sentiments always win in the end," said Orwell. "The leaders who offer blood, toil, tears, and sweat always get more out of their followers than those who offer safety and a good time." Despite what I hear from politicians and media pundits, especially those perpetual candidates and commentators both seeking better numbers in the polls, life on the road to AIDS persuades me that Orwell is right. It's that kind of leader—the kind that sweats and bleeds for victory—for whom I long.

Whenever someone asked Betty Ford what we should do with lessons we'd learned, she would say, "Do what you do best, wherever you are. Toss a pebble in the pond, and let the ripples go." In her honor, I will stick with my art. It's what I do best. My pieces carry my messages, and the messages ripple out, over time and through space and across communities. I'm not shaking the earth with powerful leadership, but I'm tossing the occasional pebble, and sometimes it matters. This week's e-mail brought a college professor's note telling me that his students have been moved by a speech I gave decades ago. A collector just called to say that he keeps my art where he sees it each morning and it reminds him of what he needs to do each day.

At such moments, I think to myself that the ripples are still breaking along the edges of my pond, my community of influence. One such ripple may yet break over a young woman of great modesty and great gifts who will become the leader we need. When she appears, she will be living evidence that our beloved American philosopher Groucho Marx was spot on: "Only one man in a thousand is a leader of men—the other 999 follow women."

9

Tell Me a Story

As a child, I learned respect for racial differences in our kitchen, manners over the dinner table, philanthropy before I could define the word. Then I was introduced to a loom— a school-room loom. That loom was soon my refuge, the place I carried harder truths. Every pain, every lonesomeness, every fear— I took each to the loom. And so I learned, decades ago, that my soul's truth emerges not from hard thought or clever conversation, but from my hands, weaving, painting, sculpting, moving.

A FEW MILLENNIA AGO, if one of us squatting at the communal fire while gnawing on the leg bone of a boar had said, "Let me tell you my life story," our fellow cavemen would have heaved bones at us. In the cave, everyone knew everyone else's story. One could have a rare private moment in such tight quarters, but not a private life. Clans and tribes may have been separated from one another by geography, language, beliefs, and customs, but every person in each community had a shared story.

Our stories are accounts of our experiences. A story isn't a lecture on numbers or a discussion of ideas; it's a narrative about what we've done, what's been done to us and with us, and what's happened as a consequence. Over time we gather chapters we are willing to publish and chapters we'd rather hide. You'll happily recount the birth of your first child, but you've spent years repressing memories of the night you were raped. Falling in love is a chapter written to violin music. Being caught shoplifting is the chapter you'll not write. And so we grow old, adding to our own stories in private if not in public. And all our stories are about not just an idea or an important song but a memorable, retellable experience: something happened, and that happening becomes part (or even the core) of a story.

The relationship between *my story* and *me* is interwoven, and inextricably so. An amnesiac doesn't know who she is, not only because she lost her purse but because she misplaced her history. It's more than lacking her driver's license or not recalling her name. Her *story* is missing. She is lost because her story has disappeared; she no longer knows what has happened in her life or what those happenings might have meant.

There is an anecdote about the first President Bush and the importance of knowing one's story—supposedly this tale takes place some months after he lost the 1992 election. He said he'd been moping about the house, feeling rejected by God and man. He had no idea what to do with himself. Finally his wife, Barbara, said, "Oh, for goodness' sake, George—stop feeling sorry for yourself! Go over to the nursing home and call on some old folks who are lonely. They'll be honored to have a visit from a president."

So the president trudged off to the health care facility where he was warmly received. He grew more cheerful with each resident's handshake or hug. He even teared up when a World War II veteran suffering cancer sat upright in his bed and saluted his president.

"The nurses asked me to make one last stop, at Sadie's room," President Bush recalled,

> *so I went in, and Sadie and I chatted for a while, but she really wasn't very interested. I mentioned that my son was governor of Texas, and she nodded. I talked about the White House, and she yawned. Finally, it occurred to me that she might not recognize me, so I said, "Sadie, do you know who I am?"*
>
> *She looked me up and down pretty good without a hint of recognition. She thought for a moment and finally said, "Nope, I sure don't."*
>
> *I was about to explain about being president when she added, "But it really don't matter. Y'all go back down the hall to the nurse's station, and they'll tell you who you are."*

Even if the account is apocryphal, it's useful in teaching us about knowing one's story. It reminds us that knowing who we are is more complicated than just knowing our names. We can give an orphan a name, but he's still an orphan. He'll still long to know who his grandfather was, whether his mother had brown eyes like his, whether the man on the corner is maybe his father. The orphan wants to know his history, his story—one that lets him know himself and explain himself to his community. Our story determines who we are, and who we are determines our story. Sadie didn't recall the name of the man visiting her, but more important, she didn't know he had been the president of the United States. His story was absent.

If the relationship between *my story* and *me* is interlocked, so is the relationship between *my story* and *my community's story*. "The Mayor's Story" tells us about the person, but also about the role that person carries out in the community; "Hap, the Town Drunk's Tale" works the same way. When I became "the Republican Lady with AIDS," one tiny virus and a single aspect of my life began to dominate my life story. It was as though I no longer was a mother, daughter, sister, friend, artist, or volunteer. Instead, I was all about AIDS. It took years for me to realize that unless I pushed back, AIDS would be the only story my community would tell about me. And if AIDS dominated my entire story, then it would define me. It was not until I discovered how little my breast cancer had defined me in the eyes of others that I realized how extensively AIDS had done so.

I recall again those women I often see after I give a speech—the ones hanging back and watching me, waiting for a chance to speak to me. Each wants to share her story, the one she doesn't trust to her community. But I can guess key elements of her story already: She's a grandmother whose beloved grandchild died of AIDS; the obituary said he had cancer, but that's just because of the shame—those closest to him know the illness had been AIDS. Or she's a woman who is infected; she's petrified to break the news to her family, her friends, her community. Whatever the women's stories may be, they are persistently dominated by a dark secret—and dominating *secret* stories will also, given time, define us.

It seems to me the reason the media doesn't do more reports on AIDS is because every editor and news director says, "We've already done that story." If there are one and a half million Americans with AIDS today, the media doesn't want to be guilty of telling the same story one and half million times. I realize the stories of those with AIDS are woven into a single, broader narrative. It's what bonds me with the women in Africa or the man in Santa Fe. We do have a shared story, multiplied in the United States by one and a half million. But it's not true that AIDS is my *whole* story, or hers, or his. We have our own tales to tell, too.

He is a man who has already been caregiver to one grandmother, two parents, two lovers, and half a dozen strangers. He now needs care himself but cannot afford it—that is some of his story. *She* is an immigrant whose husband traveled widely and had sex wantonly, but she has been ordered not to leave their rented apartment without him. She's beginning to see that what happened to her cousins is happening to her; she has AIDS. But she dares not break her husband's rule. If she does, she will be excluded forever in a land whose language she does not know, whose customs are strange, and whose regard for her is low. My story, like theirs, deals with AIDS, but our stories are not just the same, or just about AIDS.

We cannot know ourselves without knowing our stories. But what's amazing is this: Most of us cannot actually tell our own story, not in a fifteen-minute summary or a thirty-minute narrative. We recall a single event and go wandering off. We run into the night our love first blossomed, and we forget all about the clock. If you doubt me, try telling your story to yourself, or to the wall, or to this book, but tell it from beginning to end in thirty minutes or less. In recovering your story, you may be amazed at what you recover about yourself.

MY FATHER'S LIFE STORY was told in an authorized 1992 biography by Peter Golden titled *Quiet Diplomat*. The story is heavy on fact, because that's what Daddy would have wanted. He was a man who paid attention to the details even while focusing on the big picture. He craved knowledge, adored learning, loved facts. I suppose it is natural that his biography would report all the facts and tread lightly when it came to intimacy. The tenderness in my father's story was often found between the lines, out of the public eye.

By December 1994 I was feeling both the effects of the virus and the side effects of the various medicines intended to combat the virus. I was hanging in a particular limbo: that frustrating and weary place between wellness and illness, where you never feel energized but always feel guilty about lacking energy. I saw myself failing at everything that mattered, especially motherhood. My children needed more time, more laughter, more busyness than I had stamina to provide.

A few months earlier I'd agreed to a request by the American Jewish Committee to keynote a tribute for Daddy. The nearer I came to the event on my calendar, the more I wondered about the wisdom of my choice to speak. I was tired all the way down to my bones. Plus, I knew I couldn't discuss the weighty global policies that he'd negotiated, or deal with the intricate questions of borders and rights. But I imagined that this might be the last occasion I'd ever have to speak to and about him in this public way, and I wanted very much for him and others to know how grateful his children are for his loving legacy.

Paging through Peter Golden's book, I came across a passage that spoke to me, a story within the story. It gave me the boost I needed. That frigid December night in New York City, I lifted it when I spoke to my father and those who'd come to pay him homage:

In you, Daddy, we have learned something of the cost of both triumph and defeat. Above all else, we've learned that integrity outlasts both of them—and that integrity is found within ourselves, often in the meanest hour of the night.

Peter Golden captured in his biography of you the sometimes cold spirit of your father . . . and used that spirit as the backdrop to what may be the single most tender moment in the narrative.

It was January 1971. You were in Israel with my brother, Phillip, when word came that your father had died. A few days later, standing with my cousin Sherry by his coffin, you reached out and stroked your father's hair. After a moment, you said to Sherry, "Dad always liked that."

It is not clear, Daddy, whether I will stroke your hair someday, or you will stroke mine. I do not enjoy being on the road to AIDS very much, and you do not enjoy being unable to change that. But in the end, it will not matter. Because here and now, we can do something much finer than stroke hair. We can still lean over a banquet table and whisper, "I love you."

Jane and Margie, Julie and Phillip, Mom and I—we've always liked that.

134

In addition to the tight bonds of family, the legacy passed down by my parents, both of them, has been one of community-building, compassion, and justice. Daddy especially loved Detroit and poured out untold hours and dollars to strengthen its leadership and rebuild it after it had burned. Mother sees suffering and tries to alleviate it, especially when those who suffer are children, the poor, and those who've lacked opportunity.

When Daddy died, a good share of his estate was preserved to make sure that Mom is cared for. When she passes away, the bulk of what he has not already given to the Max M. and Marjorie S. Fisher Foundation will go there. Each of their children is a director of the foundation, and here our individual stories intersect. Our parents' priorities were cut into the mission and will forever guide the organization. But each of us also brings our enthusiasms. One sister champions children's health; another, the Nation of Israel. I'm enthusiastic about funding for women's health and AIDS. Remove any one of us from the board and something of our parents' enduring legacy would vanish with us. But so long as we stay together, extending our parents' legacy, we are keeping alive and growing our family's story, now engaging the third generation, including my sons, Max and Zachary.

Zack is still in college, still wondering about his gifts and interests. Max has graduated college and is already a recognized filmmaker. The company he founded is guided by his own clear vision of putting film into action to encourage service and social change. When I hear him planning documentaries, I hear familiar words that are now three generations old: *compassion, fairness, community.* And when he described his company's first feature-length documentary, I was shocked. He's doing a film on AIDS in America in the twenty-first century—as he says, "to make sure my generation doesn't become the one that drops the ball on AIDS." The family's stories grows on.

While working on his AIDS documentary, Max met a spokesperson for the Elizabeth Glaser Pediatric AIDS Foundation—the charity created by the inspiring woman who had spoken at the Democratic convention in 1992. This spokesperson was Jake Glaser, Elizabeth's son. The meeting of two sons whose mothers had spoken in the 1992 conventions offers a splendid realization that, in important ways, our story does not end even at the grave. Just as my brother and sisters and I are carrying on my parents' legacy, I realize now, I am the surviving, older generation, and Max and Jake are now discussing part of my legacy. Elizabeth has gone ahead, but Jake carries on.

Learning to tell our personal stories is important to understanding ourselves. Learning to tell our family's story is part of that—plus, it might be an interesting assignment for the next family dinner. It takes little more than a simple question: If you had to tell your family's history, where would you start and what would you say? When the laughter and bickering and contributions have ended, the family's story will have grown again.

STORYTELLING IS UNIVERSAL. Native American nations have elders whose primary task is to remember and repeat the clan's stories, conveying to young and old alike what it means to be Apache or Nez Perce. The stories offer a history of heroes and rogues, great victories and crushing defeats—all of which help define who the tribe has

IT'S IN OUR CAREGIVING

and our caretaking,

our loving and **being loved**,

which is to say in life

with others, that **we define**

ourselves and *our characters.*

become, and what it may yet be. Most cultures have their own stories, and many have storytellers. In religious traditions, priests and rabbis fill a storytelling role. Accounting for who we are as a people (or nation, tribe, religion, neighborhood, or family) involves our common story, and once we've learned that common story, we can begin putting our personal story into context.

And all these stories have power, incredible power. We see examples of this throughout our shared history as human beings. For example, countless words of debate and perhaps a million pages of rational and humane arguments had been spilled by the mid-nineteenth century over America's shameful legacy of slavery. But logic has limits, and sermons are momentary. Then a quiet woman wrote a book, *Uncle Tom's Cabin*, and in a few years and a few hundred pages this one story helped move voter sentiment enough to make it possible for President Lincoln to act.

The power of stories extends into our daily lives in unexpected ways. When I was first introduced to AA, I expected to learn a set of rules that would shake the grip of alcoholism. But AA has almost no rules. If you want to stop drinking, you may attend an AA meeting and no one may bar you. Neither may anyone tell you what to do. No one has authority over you. And here's the most amazing part: The entire program is nothing but stories—stories of people who recovered from alcoholism and how they achieved their recovery. Even the famous Twelve Steps are a common story: recollections by AA's founders of how they were transformed from dying drunks to useful citizens. Every one of the steps comes from a storytelling perspective: "we did this" and then "we did that." These steps become part of the members' common story.

Twelve step meetings are times for members to share their personal stories: what life was like, what happened, what life is like now. The first time I told my story to a group at the Betty Ford Center, my counselor, Fred Sipe, said it was a good one. Mostly, this meant he was glad I had at least tried. Using the nickname he'd assigned me, he said, "I'll tell you what, Slick: When you get honest with yourself, you're going to be amazed at your own story." Months later, having tried a good dose of that honesty, I discovered that Fred was right. In realizing that I needed to tell others my story, I learned I would need to make a clear-eyed examination of the facts myself. When I took the Fourth Step (made a "searching and fearless moral inventory" of myself), I was on my way to an honest and—as it turned out—meaningful life story.

The importance of storytelling has intersected my life at other points as well. Because I am a quilter, I've always loved the story element inherent in quilts and the quilting tradition. Because I have AIDS, the NAMES Project Foundation's AIDS Memorial Quilt has only elevated my affection for quilted stories and stories about quilts, like this one:

For more than a century the tiny community of Gee's Bend, Alabama, tucked into a curve in the Alabama River south of Selma, has told its stories through the stunning artwork in its quilts. The village has its roots in the years of slavery and reconstruction, and over the years it became one of many southern Alabama towns that time forgot. For more than a century, the women of Gee's Bend have done what women in many rural communities do: gather in quilting circles and create art. But the remote Gee's Bend quilters stayed unfamiliar with quilting styles emerging elsewhere, so they developed their own distinctive style using bold blocks of color and symmetrical patterns. When, in 2002, "The Quilts of Gee's Bend" traveled as an exhibition to the Museum of Fine Arts in Houston, the world received a special gift and I learned the story of these women.

According to legend, Gee's Bend quilters stitched patterns that were actually code language aiding runaway slaves. One Gee's Bend quilt was said to offer a map that could guide a fleeing slave in the night, across thick plantations and through river-fed swamps. Another Gee's Bend quilt taught escaped slaves what to wear when they made it "up north" or how to answer if they were questioned.

As it turns out, the story of Gee's Bend quilts steering slaves to freedom may be more myth than fact. Historians have raised hard questions, and a number of art critics have offered other, perhaps more plausible, explanations for the quilts' marvelous patterns. But it is a story so good that we want to believe it. Quilts are a universal symbol of comfort and safety; the story of a quilt needs to be a story of warmth and hope. How could anyone not be drawn to a story of quilts that did battle with slavery, fueled the hope of freedom, and offered aid to those seeking freedom?

Stories like this one, about women banding together for the good of the community, have a lesson to teach, because *believing* is precisely what gives such power to a community's judgment about our stories. If my community believes I am a hero, I am venerated; my story and my sense of self are elevated. But if my community believes, for example, that AIDS is a shameful disease, this one element of my story—the fact that I have AIDS—is like a drop of ink in a glass of water; it stains everything. If my community fears or is ashamed of my story, then almost certainly I feel the same way about it.

To the extent that we have told Americans with AIDS that theirs is a story of shame, we should ourselves be ashamed. To the extent that Americans with AIDS have believed their lives are stories that must not be told for fear of reprisal, we can measure the terrible cost paid for stigma.

I HAVE BORROWED TWO incredible stories along the road to AIDS and integrated them into my own story. Both came from older women. Both involve times that are hard. One is perfectly hysterical and one is perfectly inspiring, and both illustrate the power of story—how our stories are a recounting not of mere facts but of our experience of these facts.

The first story I've adopted occurred in 1996, a year of presidential politics, when we tend to sort people according to their party affiliations. Ever since my watershed year of 1992, I've had a hard time escaping my family's Republican roots. That was certainly true four years later when I was invited to speak at an event in Little Rock, Arkansas, just as the presidential campaign involving a particular hometown favorite—a Democrat—was heating up.

Out of the few hundred people attending the event, I was one of perhaps two Republicans. Everyone was being very discreet. No one mentioned politics or party loyalties. No one, that is, until community awards were being handed out, and the final recipient said she wanted to talk.

I've told this story dozens of times since, and it has never needed embellishing. The award winner was an elderly public health nurse—bright, quick, seventy-seven years old, and wonderfully feisty. She bounced up to the podium and looked me in the eye with a *You ain't gonna stop me, lady* stare. Then she took the microphone from me and opened with—and I quote—"I've had it with them dumb Republicans."

Every politically correct person took a sharp breath as the award winner made her point:

WE MUST *accept ourselves* if we are to **accept** others.

For fifteen years I've talked to them dumb Republicans. Over and over, I've explained there ain't but three ways you can get AIDS: swap needles or blood, have sex, or get born with it. And for fifteen years, them dumb Republicans kept askin', "Cain't you get it from mosquitoes?"

I'm telling y'all right now that from now on, I'm gonna tell 'em, "Yep, you can get it from mosquitoes. But only in three states: Florida, Louisiana, and Arkansas. 'Cause them's the only states mosquitoes grow so big, them Republicans can have sex with 'em.

The Mosquito Story has traveled with me since that night, not only because it's funny but because it's a powerful story. It lampoons ignorance and fear. It reduces those who are judgmental to the role of village dunce. It makes ridiculous with humor what others have made ridiculous with meanness. It has power to make us laugh at what should be truly laughable.

The other story is the account of Mother Pollard, as told by Taylor Branch in his magnificent story of America in the final years of Dr. Martin Luther King, *Parting the Waters*. The Mother Pollard Story first became part of my own as I was finishing my first memoir in 1994 and an enormous wave of weariness washed over me. I recounted hours of weary grief spent over the death of first one friend, then another:

> *The accumulation of deaths wears us down, like sandpaper rubbed relentlessly into our raw flesh. It isn't just the pain that ruins us; it's the bone-tired weariness of dealing with the pain. It's what makes me want to stop, especially to stop giving speeches in which I'm expected to raise other people's hopes.*

I was talking about a tiredness so intense that it paralyzes us. But I wanted the book to share an encouraging message, especially to the two readers of the book who I believed would most need encouragement: my sons. I expected to be dead long before they entered high school or grew old enough to tackle the things I was writing about. And I wanted them to know that when we are worn, we do not give up. So I told the story of Mother Pollard:

> *Early in 1956, the Alabama bus boycott was failing. No laws had changed; no buses had been integrated. No one was suffering except those who walked.*
>
> *Then came a little-known hero from Montgomery's African-American community, Mother Pollard. For untold decades she had cared for the sick and raised the orphans, black and white alike. Now, in her waning years, Mother Pollard joined the boycott and walked. As the days stretched to weeks, and then months, she walked. When the winter weather worsened, and she began to slip and fall, against*

140

the advice of King and others, she would pick herself up, time after time, and walk.

A meeting was called to consider ending the boycott and finding another means of protest. The crowd was divided between speeches and arguments until Mother Pollard rose to speak.

"I would rather crawl on my knees than ride on a bus," she told the hushed and now embarrassed crowd. She spoke of years of humiliation, of self-hatred, of injustice and shame. She noted that the outcome would have little to do with her life, but much to do with the lives of her many children. And then she gave the entire civil rights movement one of its classic refrains when she concluded, "My feets is tired, but my soul is rested."

Especially at those times when I felt most like a fading, failing mother who belonged at home with her sons, not in some distant city answering a cub reporter's ill-advised questions, I would remember Mother Pollard.

I've been given the world's finest medical care. No prescription has been denied me. When I am exhausted, I can afford to hire help. But when I am bone-weary, so tired that I genuinely wonder about going on, I don't reach for a pill or a helper. I reach for a story—a potent, humbling story.

And when I think of my own life story—even now, with the boys grown, with me propped up by miracles of every kind, moving with hope through the challenges of cancer—even now I sometimes imagine that when I am gone, some kindly stranger will bend low and whisper to the boys, "Your mother has not gone, Max, she has merely gone ahead. Her body grew tired, Zack . . . but her soul is rested."

In the end, it's all about our story.

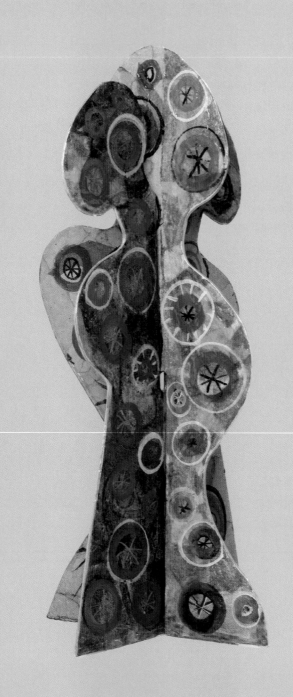

10

Finding My Voice

CURIOUS SOUL

Some artists see what they will create and then they create it. It has never been that way for me. I come with curiosity more than vision, a question more than an answer. When I create a satisfying work—and not all satisfy, especially some days!—I will see in the final piece, for the first time, what I wanted to express. My mute soul will have spoken on the canvas or in the quilt. I'll stand back, look, and realize that my soul's curiosity has been fulfilled.

I'VE ALWAYS MOVED FROM one home to another with a purpose. When, in 1985, I left first Rancho Mirage, California (the Betty Ford Center), and then Florence, Colorado (extended treatment at Parkside Lodge), I headed back to New York City. I'd been there for a few years, and it felt like home. It felt like the place I could develop as an artist.

I'd come to accept the existence of a Higher Power while at the Betty Ford Center, and that acceptance blossomed into a reliable sense of Divinity while I was at Parkside. Before Parkside, I would have said that I *believed* in a Supernatural Reality. After Parkside, I could say that I had *experienced* that Reality. Since those days in the Colorado mountains, I have never wondered whether being spiritual matters to me. It matters.

It was at Parkside that I also began to understand that I could communicate through my art. Although I still cringe a little when I hear myself say, "I'm an artist," I think it's true. As I wrote in my earlier memoir, "Finding art was a critical step in the direction of finding myself," and it happened at Parkside. My artwork is my voice. Finding one's voice is very close to finding one's self.

A pianist who suffers a great loss might go to the piano to express otherwise inexpressible grief, because it's on the keyboard that she can be most articulate. In the range of notes and chords and accents, she can give herself over to potent, pounding grief.

When my eyes and hands are at work creating a piece of visual art, it is my *most articulate moment. I may not even know my feelings or beliefs or thoughts until I've seen what I am producing. I begin a work not knowing what to hope for, except an honest expression that will flow from my soul. And then my hands and eyes—and heart—take over; I sketch, I mold, I paint. As the piece nears completion, I finally stand up straight, realizing that my back hurts from the long period of leaning. I get my own first look at what's happened, what's been created. And then, for the first time, I say to myself,* Oh, yes—that's right. *That's exactly what I'm feeling, that's just what I believe, that's precisely what I hope. Until that moment, I honestly will not . . . have known. It's as if I meet myself, discover myself, in my artwork.*

Back in New York in 1986 I reconnected with designer and artist Brian Campbell. We'd known each other before I became clean and sober. Given the changes in my life, I needed to tell Brian I wasn't certain I could spend time with him. When he said, "I think I want what you've got," and acted on that claim by getting into his own recovery program, the door swung open to a richer relationship than we could possibly have known in the past.

Brian had technical skills that were amazing; I wanted to study them. And he had a certain confidence, not a swagger or arrogance but a genuine delight in having a designer's flair; I wished I could work in public with his sense of ease. Soon we were working together, playing together, falling in love together.

One night I was trying to explain to Brian that I felt as though art was my vocabulary, my speech, my way of letting out what was in my soul. He pulled from his wallet a worn slip of paper on which he'd written this quotation from American sculptor David Smith: "Art is made from dreams and visions, and things not known, and least of all from things that can be said. It comes from the inside of who you are, when you face yourself." By the time Brian looked up, I was crying.

Hearing Brian read those words was one of the most memorable events in my life. I knew, in that instant, that I had been a mute all my life, full of wishes and hurts and hopes and unknowable things that I could not express. A brief quotation convinced me I was not crazy—a stranger named David Smith knew exactly what I felt. I'd been taught speech and writing, which are fine for "things that can be said." But when it came to those agonies and glories that inhabit my depths, words failed me. I needed another way, and there was another way: art.

When I have a speech to give, I share my soul's thoughts with a trusted friend who helps assemble sentences and paragraphs; when it's ready, I give the speech. But when I am in my studio, working on art, I need no intermediary. No one needs to be my soul's translator. My heart goes directly onto the canvas, into the paper, throughout the quilt. My soul feels for the texture we need, it searches for the best color, it senses the right size.

For three decades art has been the constant in my life. I was forming wet paper into sculpture before Max was formed in my womb, before marriage, before AIDS. In thirty years of moves—from New York to Florida to Washington, DC, to Nyack to Florida again and now to Sedona—the one constant in every place has been my studio. Though sometimes it has been no more than a portion of one room, my studio has been my sanctuary. I go there to meet friends and to make things to sell and to work. But I also go there on a spiritual quest, to find out what my soul has to say now.

THE FALL OF 1995 roared into the house I'd leased on the outskirts of Washington, DC. The world was returning to Washington after the summer months, when legislators and staff go home and the city is entrusted to the tender mercies of tourists. The boys were starting school, so mornings had morphed from sleepy summer moments into the noisy chaos of lost shoes and "How'd he get dirty so fast?" I was busy planning dinners with VIPs, because I'd relocated from Florida to have access to political and scientific leaders whose decisions would shape the future of AIDS in America. Early in the summer, I had been honored to accept an invitation from the United States Senate's Committee on Rules and Administration to display a one-woman art exhibit, the first ever, in the Russell Rotunda come September. In a matter of just weeks, all the pieces needed to be finished, photographed, crated, and made ready for viewing.

The exhibit invitation thrilled me. My art would stand alone for five days in the Senate's great hall amid the marble statues of the republic's heroes. Being the first woman to have a one-person exhibit here was like being placed in history. I was humbled, delighted, frightened, and grateful. While we worked feverishly in my garage-converted-into-a-studio, I reminded everyone that this had been the goal: *Let my art tell the story.*

With the invitation to create the exhibit had come an opportunity to name the collection. I chose *MESSAGES: Recent Paintings and Sculpture.* Some of the sculpture and handmade paper were installed on or in symbolic shapes (a window, a door, a podium, and so forth). The exhibit's brochure explained that "we look through a window; from a podium, we deliver our message; slam a door in our face, we may come back another way. Working on a window or podium or door is finding a symbol which delivers part of my message even before I begin work."

Congressional leaders from both parties rallied to endorse the September 25–29 show. Senators Orrin Hatch, Nancy Kassebaum, and Ted Kennedy agreed to host an artist's reception, and fifteen other senators and representatives signed on as sponsors. Those who knew me only as "the Republican lady with AIDS" noted that, although Senator Robert

Dole was among the sponsors, it was Senator Ted Kennedy who drafted the Senate's statement:

> *This exhibit has been praised nationally and internationally for what it teaches: the value of human life, the urgency of human dignity, and the joy of human community. Mary Fisher's life and work are models of courage that knows no boundary of gender or faith, partisanship, or nationality—in her presence, we are all learners. What she teaches is a truth that could change the world.*

The Senate had been, at best, a reluctant actor in the American AIDS drama; by inviting my exhibit, this important institution finally affirmed the magnitude of AIDS in America. Bipartisanship was a powerful statement in the midst of a plague that had so divided the parties. Government was, in this one symbolic act, offering a message of its own. I was grateful that I'd been judged worthy of this honor as an artist. To be sure that the drama of the opening was preserved, we kept the exhibit private, not giving advance peeks or photographs before we stationed the pieces throughout the Russell Rotunda.

147

Ten days before the exhibit opened, I was disappointed (but not shocked) to learn that the *Washington Times* had published a small but nasty piece characterizing my work, which no one from the newspaper had ever seen, as "controversial" and "bizarre." *The Times* had been founded in 1982 by the Reverend Sun Myung Moon, Korean founder of the Unification Church. Thanks to his considerable wealth and right-wing political clout, Moon's paper had gained over the years in both subscribers and influence, and it was frequently quoted by conservatives as if it had the objective veracity of other newspapers.

When Senators called, asking about this "controversial" and "bizarre" artwork, I sent photographs. I wrote Senator John Warner, chair of the inviting committee, to assure him "vigorously" that "the exhibit is not political, partisan, or disrespectful of life or death; it does not play lightly with the pain of the disease, or sacrifice the dignity of the United States Senate." I reminded Senator Warner that no one, including the *Washington Times,* had even seen the exhibit. And I added, "If you are concerned about the character of either my work or me, please come see the work while it is still in my studio. I would be honored by your presence."

Senator Warner didn't visit. The exhibit was scheduled to open on a Monday morning. But the Friday before, as the truck loaded with the exhibit pieces waited to carry them from the studio to the Senate building, he faxed a letter saying that because another senator had objected, the exhibit was off.

It turns out the objection was to one sculpture, a coffin around which I'd scrolled a line from one of my speeches: *Let us unite in life rather than in death.* The piece was central to the exhibit because it established the life-and-death character of the virus I, and so many others, carry. But the United States Senate, which votes on Articles of War and addresses life-and-death issues on a routine agenda, wanted an exhibit dealing with AIDS that didn't suggest that everyone with AIDS was dying.

Monday morning, September 25, the sun rose over Washington, DC—and the opening of the exhibit. The Carpenters Union Building, two blocks from the Russell Building, had opened space over the weekend, and we had set up the entire exhibit in time for the *TODAY* show to open with a live feed within the exhibition. Visually, the television shots were stunning: Viewers could see the exhibit and, through the expansive windows, the Senate building from which the exhibit had been expelled. *USA Today* ran a front-page note and a longer, inside story remarking, among other things, that Senator Warner "could not be reached for comment." Late Monday, five of Senator Warner's colleagues—Republican senator Orrin Hatch, Democratic senators Dingell and Kennedy, and House members (and Republicans) Steve Gunderson and Fred Upton—sent all House and Senate members a letter inviting them to a *MESSAGES* reception, describing the work as "sensitive and inspirational."

Two (Republican) Presidential Libraries subsequently invited the complete *MESSAGES* exhibit to be on display and asked that I open these exhibits with keynote remarks. At the Gerald R. Ford Presidential Library and Museum in Michigan I observed that, since being expelled from the Senate, the exhibit had been more warmly welcomed in "controversial settings like the Ford Museum." I added that "the materials arrived here from that well-known liberal bastion of the West: the Richard Nixon Memorial Library and Birthplace."

Nearly twenty years have passed since the flap over a box with words on it. One lesson I drew from the expelled exhibit is that art has a power words alone may not convey. Nothing was "controversial" or "bizarre"

148

when I said, in a widely heard and widely published speech, that Americans needed to put down prejudice and come together, uniting "in life rather than in death." But when I sculpted that line along the edge of the coffin, the message became offensive. My polite request was, by its placement in a new setting as part of a piece of art, turned into a howling cry. In a speech, the line was acceptable; in a piece of art, it slashed at some senator's sense of decency.

Another, more personal lesson concerned my belief that I could speak to those at the highest levels of political power, and they would listen. I had moved to the Washington area with an optimism conceived in my father's home and nurtured by my time in the Ford White House. My optimism had been ratified by the invitation to become the first woman in American history to have a solo exhibit in the Senate's Russell Rotunda. It took only one planted story in the *Washington Times*, one senator's discomfort with the truth, and one faxed letter from a committee chairman to expose my optimism for what it was: naïveté. Several senators and representatives had, as individuals, endorsed and even promoted the exhibit; but the institution itself had, through its officers, rejected *MESSAGES*.

After gladly accepting the invitation to give the opening lecture when the Nixon Library hosted the exhibit in spring 1996, I grew too ill to fly to California. The lecture was released in paper form instead, under the title "Private Artists and Public Art," and included my conviction that "art is, as nearly as I can tell, all about the truth":

> *The language of artists is a language very much like the language of religion. Artists speak of reaching into their souls, of listening for God, of being given visions, of dreading the truth they need to show to others. The world of art echoes with the language of the ancient prophets. And I must tell you that some of the most spiritually focused and joyful moments of my life have been when God and I were making art together. . . .*
>
> *W. H. Auden, the poet, introduced his last collection of poems with a wonderful, confessional Foreword in which he publicly apologized for having earlier published some "dishonest" poetry. "A dishonest poem," he wrote, "is one which expresses,* no matter how well, *feelings or beliefs which the author never felt or entertained . . . One must be honest even about one's prejudices. . . ."*

And then, with my senatorial experience clearly in mind, I added this:

Those who observe the artist's work must allow the truth to be spoken. My earlier ancestors in the tribes of Israel had the unpleasant characteristic of stoning prophets when they announced a truth the people did not like. And one wonders if such stonings are finished, even in our own day.

Wisdom

is the ability

to live

by trust

when we have

no answers.

I was, and I remain, grateful to those who welcomed and protected the *MESSAGES* exhibit both in Washington, DC, and on the road. No one stoned me. But when I thumb through the clippings and memories of late September 1995, I remember feeling, as a person with AIDS, isolated, rejected, outraged. We *were*, for God's sake, all dead or dying! How could my soul produce art without acknowledging death?

We had moved the exhibit to preserve it, but the hurt of the rejection was not erased. I felt discounted as a person of worth, perhaps as a woman, certainly as a Republican. I imagined that if I'd been a better artist, the exhibit would have been retained; it would have "worked." I had refused to allow politics to censor my exhibit, so politicians cancelled my exhibit and went home for dinner—just another day on the Hill.

Within a year, my family had left the Washington suburbs and gone looking for happiness in a small town far from the Russell Rotunda.

WHEN I'VE SPOKEN TO other artists about what generates their creativity, what happens within them that inspires or enables them to create, I nearly always get the same response: a blank stare.

I understand. I've never been able to explain it either. The David Smith quote Brian carried with him says art "comes from the inside of who you are, when you face yourself." But in what possible sense does "facing yourself" turn into art?

I can describe my experience better than I can explain it. I'll be in my studio—puttering, organizing a drawer, sorting through materials—when I sense that something is being restrained inside me. I suppose this is where it starts—where I turn to face *me*. I have to settle myself, calm down a bit, force myself into taking one step at a time. But I'm edgy, eager. I've said before that "I feel like I'm on fire with the idea," even before I know what the idea is. I'm energized. I don't need food and I can't sleep. I want to say something I've never said before in a language that needs no words. And from these moments—sometimes within minutes, sometimes over the course of days—come designs, patterns, sculptures, photographs, colors, portraits, all the things that once filled my soul and now fill my studio.

Not being a theologian, I can't define the Divine. My Jewish tradition warns me against even attempting to name "G-d." But my experience tells me that being creative is deeply godlike. The opening chapters of Scripture are the Story of Creation, and we are behaving like ("in the image of") the Creator when we ourselves are creative. We may say, "The spirit moved me." It's an accurate description. The link between spirituality and art is real, tangible, common. I've experienced it.

As art and spirituality are joined, so are art and healing. I was invited to speak to that theme—art and healing—in the fall of 2007 at an annual reception at Sedona's marvelous Goldenstein Gallery, where a collection of my works was offered for sale. I was feeling quite well then, and I spoke with considerable confidence. I recalled my speech at the Republican convention as an experience during which "I was inspired. I had a purpose in what seemed like a senseless waste of human life. And when we find purpose, we are mending that which has broken us. I was healing." I spoke of the process of creating as, for me,

a process of healing, for the same reason that cradling [an] African orphan is healing, and urging a congressman to lead with courage is healing, and warning young adults that danger is stalking them is healing. It is all healing because it all enables us to mend what is broken within ourselves and between ourselves. Visual and tactile art are rivers that flow directly from the soul, unimpeded by sentence structure and verbal syntax. [Art] has a force that spoken language cannot quite muster.

If you see my art today and compare it to what I was producing ten or fifteen years ago, you'll see a new dimension: It has a future. The horizon is farther in the distance; themes that speak to the future are now authentically mine. I find more light that is un-shadowed, more colors that testify to hope, more textures and shapes that lean outward and forward. With the future as part of my reality, my soul can reach beyond darkness and speak to tomorrow. It's very life-affirming, very healing.

During interviews in the first few years after my HIV diagnosis, I claimed that AIDS had not impacted my art. If the interviewer persisted, I'd deflect questions with one of my own: "What does AIDS look like?" That usually stopped the interviewer. But fifteen years later, I had realized that AIDS had indeed found my soul and was a part of my story, my identity. The soul could no more express itself without acknowledging the AIDS than I could create a Senate exhibit dealing with AIDS but avoiding any mention of death. The healing process had seeped into my creative process, and the tangible evidence was my artwork.

I was invited back to the Goldenstein Gallery for this event on several succeeding years. Twelve months after my first speech at the gallery, I offered what is easily the most extensive statement I ever made about the crossroads where my life, my art, and my healing meet:

What's become clearer and clearer to me . . . is that those who attempt art do so with their whole selves. It isn't just our eyes or our ears or our hands. It has to do with the entire human experience, the power of hormones as well as headaches, whatever makes me giggle and whatever makes me weep. It is my soul's response to life as I experience it . . . and it has always been this way for artists: the young woman in the death camp who sketched butterflies, the young man who uses graffiti and rap to show his rage at injustices, the great Mahalia Jackson starting into "Swing Low, Sweet Chariot" when she had been banned, for her color, from the White House. . . .

In my own case, my art gives me a way to speak about the unspeakable. It allows me to remember and express the feeling of holding Brian's hand as he died and of cuddling the infant orphan who never had a fighting chance. It provides the voice in which I can express my horror at the ravages of poverty, my shock at the resilience of racism, my laughter at the goofy look on my dog's face, my contentment at the end of a quiet day measuring the beauty of Sedona.

Art is no more able to be disconnected from our lives than is the concept of "wellness." I am not well if I have a perfect body but an agonized spirit. Think of how unwell the teenage athlete was who, despite a perfect body, fumbled what would have been the winning touchdown before the hometown crowd; he hung himself in his family's basement. He was not well. Or conversely, think of how well Monet was in his waning years, cataracts covering his eyes, still able to feel the color of his beloved water lilies, still blending that distinctive yellow that cries out of sunshine and egg yolk and mystery. Ailing, but still well . . .

What I have heard in the cries of dying infants at Mother Teresa's on the edge of Lusaka has taken root in my heart and has found its way into my art. What I have seen in the eyes of my children and the hopes of my mother; what I've smelled in the early-morning Sedona kitchen but also the unrefrigerated morgue where African bodies are stacked; what I have touched, from the chill of a cold drink to the raging fever of a child's suffering, from the gentle curve of a red Sedona rock to the razor's edge of a cutting tool; what I have tasted, and touched, and smelled, and seen, and heard—all of my senses have taken in the magic of art, the mystery of a language that does not need verbs and nouns to communicate.

Fast-forward one more year. It was now 2009, and I was back again, speaking at the Goldenstein Gallery. As if to prove the truth of the previous year's remarks—"those who attempt art do so with their whole selves"—my whole self had grown reticent, and I was "less and less inclined to allow my art to put my soul on public display." I did not yet know, and could not have known, that I was just two months away from being hospitalized for a gripping depression triggered by side effects from an HIV drug. But what I could not know intellectually or rationally, my soul knew experientially, instinctually. "My studio still lures me," I confessed, but "what I am doing is more and more done because I cannot *not* do art." In my art, I was still expressing all that I experienced, "even if I'm unwilling to have it hauled into public."

I knew that my soul was still being expressed through my art. I couldn't shut it off. So I was folding up and inward. I was hiding. But I also knew that my art was revealing more than I wanted revealed. *Seeing* it was difficult enough; *showing* it was dangerous. I wanted to hide.

MANY YEARS AGO, I was awaiting a visit from the always brilliant and sometimes biting *New York Times* columnist Frank Rich. As I sat in my studio, it came to me in a flash, in a panic: the vast difference between producing art and exhibiting art. Putting your soul's work on display, this act of aesthetic and personal nakedness, is what distinguishes the professional from the amateur, the artist from the hobbyist. But it's not for the faint of heart—going public with your soul is a grueling and terrifying experience.

As I once told students at the Rochester Institute of Technology's College of Imaging Arts and Sciences, "If you believe you are an artist, that is enough: You are."

> *Your art may win you fame, or it may never win a single award or recognition. You may have international exhibits, or you may have your work stored in the back of your neighbor's garage. I don't care, and I wish you would not care either. Because if you believe you have a message within you that, with training and time and hard work, you can translate into a human form that others can see or hear or touch—do it. Because that is the essence of being an artist.*

I never want to say that I love art more than I love anything else, because it isn't true. I love my children, and I would give up my art for them. But were I forced to make that trade, my sons would have a hollow, mute mother. When I found art, I found my voice. By allowing my soul to speak through my art, I am constantly learning who I am. Of all life's discoveries, this is among the most precious: to know myself.

And when I dare to show you my art, you discover who I am, too.

As Shakespeare's Hamlet said, "Ah, there's the rub!" *Seeing* my art delights me with new discoveries; *showing* my art terrifies me with new risks. To make the art, I must be creative; to show you the art, I must be vulnerable.

Should you drop by my studio someday, you would be warmly welcomed. But here's the unwritten rule: If you do not like what you see, be civil. My art is my soul's offspring, my heart's child. Showing it to you is like holding out my naked newborn for your inspection. You do not need to buy my art, any more than you need to adopt my child. But you may not tell me I have an ugly baby.

11

Seeing Life Upside-Down

─────────── **MAGIC SOUL** ───────────

I've seen men whose legs were torn off in war, giggling at the antics of their 3-year-old daughters. Magic. It's a magical laughter that falls out of their souls. I've known widows whose faces shed 30 years when a caring man asked them to dance, children who defied a playground bully, beggars whose children attended Harvard. Neither the odds nor reasonable explanations will explain this away. To understand, we must remember this: Our souls can do magic, and they do.

SHORTLY AFTER I SPOKE at the 1992 Republican convention, I began receiving invitations to speak at worship services—to "preach," of all things. After recovering from the shock, I accepted a few engagements only to discover that the experience was incredible, not at all what I had expected, even life-sustaining. Preparation could be reflective, preaching had rules that were different from just speaking to an audience, and after-worship conversations were often amazing and memorable. One big difference between giving a speech and preaching was the context: People came to hear something meaningful. And a sermon invited me to go places and say things I couldn't politely touch in most settings. Just saying "AIDS" was enough to gag most conversations. Add "gay" and "dying," and you were into a strained conversation about sex and religion. Politics were divisive. News reports were angry. Science was uncertain. But the pulpit was a safe place from which to speak the truth.

In the context of a worship service, where we try to find our place in the universe, in a spiritual life, in a storied tradition, AIDS could be understood as a fundamentally human and moral issue. It wasn't about screaming protestors or ugly slurs; it was about suffering and lonesomeness, brokenness and reconciliation, how we love and how we pray. It was about life on the road to death. Raising questions and pointing toward answers about life's meaning—even asking whether life *had* meaning—was possible here, perhaps even expected. In speeches, I tried to be sane and rational; in sermons, I needed only to be sane. Rather than start with logic or fact, I could start from a premise of faith, or belief, or "things not seen," and I wouldn't be failing my audience.

In other words, in the pulpit, life could start from a whole different place. Here, the poor could inherit the earth; the downtrodden could be closest to God; the rich and powerful would be held to account, while the suffering and dying received their due. In the pulpit, I could see life upside down: beggars triumphing over kings, and spiritual questions trumping material goods.

One of the first invitations to preach came from a large Presbyterian church in New Jersey. Recognizing that I had relatively little religious connection to this congregation—I had no training in theology and had been raised in a Jewish family—I knew I needed something to break the ice. Happily, I found that Mark Twain was able to provide the line I needed, in his opening to "A Dog's Tale," a 1903 *Harper's* article written in the voice of a puppy: "My father was a St. Bernard, my mother was a collie, but I am a Presbyterian."

Like Twain's puppy, I am a product of my parents and yet somehow a different species altogether. The Judaism of my first home in Louisville had been largely ethnic and social: Yiddish slogans, Jewish jokes, and a joyful sense that we belonged together. I don't think I truly understood that there were people who weren't Jews until I approached school age.

The Judaism I experienced growing up in Detroit was more communal than familial. We were part of the broader Jewish community there. But Judaism in our home was heavily political and philanthropic. It was not a day-to-day issue of spirituality, let alone religion. We were, most of the time, what others politely called "nonobservant." There was a seder at Passover, and I learned enough Hebrew to survive. But we were of the Jewish culture, not religious Jews. My father led us into our concepts of Judaism with his unquestioned support for Israel and his total commitment to philanthropy—for Jews and non-Jews alike—giving away what he'd been given. He considered his material achievements humbly, as something he'd received rather than earned. He would say that we need to "give back to the community because they gave to us."

My community as I grew into a young woman was Kingswood, the "Cranbrook school for girls," and it was ecumenical. The school's history was rooted in old Anglican and Episcopalian traditions. We prayed at certain special events, and someone needed to carry a cross down the aisle for graduation. The honor of cross-bearing fell to the class president, and at my graduation, that person was me. I was allowed to carry the nation's flag instead of the cross. The flag was awkward to carry, but the cross was heavier. If others expected that this would make me uneasy, that I would feel like a stranger here, I didn't know it. Whenever I ventured into the campus sanctuary, I found myself comforted by the surroundings. I liked the smells, the oldness, the sounds of liturgical songs and a priest's chanting. It felt good to me, safe.

In both Louisville and Detroit, the sense I had of the truly spiritual was owing to my mother's influence. She had, and has, an absolute belief in what we cannot see but do experience. I'm reluctant to describe her convictions, because I want to be fair to her—I don't want to undervalue what she has given to me. She is not overtly religious, does not regularly attend worship, and keeps a broad range of religious icons in her life. But

I have long **believed** that

life has purpose

AND MY HIV+ STATUS

has not changed this

CONVICTION.

she has an open mind to almost any report of a "spiritual experience," whether her own or that of someone she trusts, and she lives convinced that the material world is no more than one aspect of our existence. She reads philosophers and entertains spiritual leaders. She's comfortable with the ideas of reincarnation and regeneration, with hearing the voice of a bygone parent, with seeing evidence of the Divine in everything from a budding flower to a wayward grandchild. She is deeply spiritual.

My version of spirituality has flourished later in life. As a young adult I went "looking for myself" in Israel. I lived there, worked there, and did not find myself there. I came back to the United States and continued the search here. Eventually, I was introduced to myself at the Betty Ford Center, where I was also introduced to the writings of Bill Wilson, cofounder of Alcoholics Anonymous.

"Bill W." described his own transformation from terminal alcoholic to global leader as the result of a white-light experience of the Divine. What he created (along with "Dr. Bob," his cofounder) is a program of sobriety that is self-consciously spiritual. "The spiritual life is not a theory," he wrote. And through the nearly forty years of his sobriety and writing, he continually focused not on creed or dogma but on experience. For him, spirituality is the recognition that we have within ourselves of a "spirit" that is satisfied when aligned with the Spirit of the Universe (or if you prefer, the Spirit of God). Once we sense that there is a Power greater than ourselves, and give ourselves to that Power, we will let go of our self-will and act in concert with the will of "a God of our own understanding" who will teach us to love. While AA is rigorously nonreligious, it is also fundamentally spiritual.

Several years after the teachings of AA began shaping my spiritual life, so did psychiatrist and philosopher Dr. Brian Weiss. Though he had become famous as the author of regression (or past-life) therapy, Brian helped me to focus not on past lives but on *this* life, showing me how to integrate spirituality into everything that mattered to me: my sense of purpose, my new role in motherhood, my work as an artist, and eventually, my AIDS journey.

In difficult and what might have been dangerous times of my life, Brian's humble wisdom infused me with the conviction that although at certain moments it might not feel as if life had meaning or purpose, it did. The evidence seemed to say I had no value and no future; Brian persuaded me that I had both. His message seemed to say, *You're an artist? Let's use art for this purpose.* Or, *Children? A wonderful way to serve.* And then there was AIDS? *Okay, that's a surprise, but let's see it as a new opportunity.* Brian was teaching me to turn things upside down, to convert problems into opportunities, grief into grace.

What I offered up at the Republican National Convention in Houston in 1992 was a speech, not a sermon. It was delivered in the most political of all settings. But for me, it was an opportunity to serve with a spiritual message. Within the first sixty seconds I had practically aped the language of both Bill W. and Brian Weiss:

> *I bear a message of challenge, not self-congratulation. I want your attention, not your applause. I would never have asked to be HIV-positive. But I believe that in all things there is a purpose, and I stand before you and before the nation, gladly.*

My sense that life comes with a purpose has been strengthened more recently through time spent with a humble Brazilian man, now nearing seventy years of age. I was first introduced to Joao Teixeira de Faria by a friend in Sedona who had gone to Brazil to meet this "John of God."

Based on this friend's testimony, I wound up meeting Joao when he visited the United States in the fall of 2008. In a world of televised ministries making flamboyant claims and raising obscene amounts of money, this spiritual servant, I had been told, was the real deal: honest, pure, and mystical. I was uncertain what this meeting would be like.

What I found was a man of simple tastes and appearance, a man with modest formal education, who sews his own plain clothes and says that God offers hope for healing of body, mind, and soul. He has never deviated from his fundamental claim that only God offers healing and hope. Joao asks for nothing, not even a contribution, and encourages those who will listen to "respect one another and love God above all else. Love resolves everything." This message struck home with me. Since our first meeting, I've visited Joao three times in Brazil.

Someone in AA once reflected on his own life and concluded that "religion is for people who are afraid of going to hell; spirituality is for those who have been there." I am not a spiritual model or a leader to be followed. I am, and may always be, a seeker. In the tradition of my mother, I continue to look and listen and wonder. Perhaps I sound like Pollyanna. A strict rationalist might question my claim of sanity. But living life upside down works for me. Listening to Joao's message, I'm at peace with AIDS, with cancer, with aging, with myself. I sleep well. And I wake to the certainty that healing is ours for the asking, miracles happen, and my life will have all the meaning I allow it to have—so long as I act on respect for others more than for myself and remember that love resolves everything.

KNOWING WE ARE GOING to become very sick, and then we are going to die, is a hard slap at our spirituality. I remember driving to Brian Weiss's office in the wake of my 1991 diagnosis. My hands were on the wheel, my eyes were on the road, and my mind was in a funeral home looking at caskets. I did not feel spiritual. I felt sad.

The two hardest realities of dying, for me, were the aloneness and the finality. I would, eventually, be alone. Although others could be with me in my illness, when the moment of death arrived, I would have already let go of their hands. My children would be orphans and I would be dead.

And the aloneness would be permanent. It would be over. Final. Kaput. This did not seem like, in Brian's words, an "opportunity."

But this was not unique to me: We're all going to die. I'd always known I would die. So what had changed? I now knew (or thought I knew) the *how* and the *when* of my dying. Death had become a tangible reality in my immediate future: It would come soon, and it would come by AIDS. It took only one last thing—just a drop of self-pity—for these realities to arouse a sense of injustice. It wasn't fair. I was one of those who would die before I was "supposed to." The timing was awful, and the only thing worse was the process: I was going to die slowly and miserably, in the company of others who had been stigmatized, while the rest of America went on its merry way, not caring. This seemed to be the reality of AIDS.

On November 8, 1992, sixteen months after I was diagnosed, I delivered a sermon at Church of the Valley in Van Nuys, California. Decades have passed since I stepped into that pulpit, yet I can remember the feeling of it, the sense of injustice that came with the red ribbon I wore as I spoke about the grief I and others were experiencing:

> *Because the epidemic first surfaced in America within gay communities, this grief has been compounded. Old patterns of discrimination came to life with new brutality. Traditional sources of comfort— the home and the church—became, instead, tribunals of judgment. Parents rejected children. Young men, untrained in nursing skills, cared first for dying friends and then died themselves, alone— because the homes from which they had come were now closed to them. Voices rang out from pulpits, saying the virus was God's idea, speculating that HIV was divine retribution. Intimate messages of rejection were matched by public policies of indifference. Not until the virus jumped all social fences, putting all of us at risk, did the nation respond. Our response was fueled by self-interest more than compassion. In the end, the HIV/AIDS community was blanketed with a grief too deep for consolation.*

The AIDS community was, in fact, on a death march, and we frequently marched past churches. Here I was, engaged in a deeply spiritual act (preaching) in a perfectly religious setting (Christian worship), and I found myself in the uncomfortable position of needing to acknowledge that religion had been an unreliable friend of AIDS in America.

> *For the HIV/AIDS community in America, the voice of God heard from communities of faith has been terribly muted. Temples should have raised high the roof beams to bring them in; churches should have shouted messages of grace from the rooftop. But what most members of the HIV/AIDS family have heard is whispers about their morality and the hope that, like modern-day lepers, they will not get too close. And so the peculiar grief has grown, fed by shame and ignorance, stigma and rejection.*

Despite what I was saying about our collective grief, after more than a year of dealing with my diagnosis, aided by time with Brian Weiss and others, I had begun to sense that the spiritual solution to my own grief was within reach. I needed only to separate myself from those who used religion as a weapon against others. Against me. Against us.

> *To suggest that the God of Scripture hurls HIV and AIDS at his children is profanity. To imagine that some of us are more worthy of grace than others is hypocrisy. There is nothing in ourselves that earns grace, else it is not grace at all. Because grace is love undeserved. Grace is the rescue we can't perform, the comfort we can't grasp.*

The chaos of those early months of living with the diagnosis had largely, if imperfectly, settled into a quieter acceptance of the facts: I had AIDS. I would, at some point, die. I could fight, whine, or scramble after every preposterous "cure," or I could become willing to accept the reality and find meaning in it. It was this acceptance that Brian Weiss encouraged me to accomplish and, before him, that I'd learned in AA when I stood in a meeting, holding hands, reciting Reinhold Niebuhr's prayer: "God grant me the serenity to accept the things I cannot change . . . ." Once I acknowledged that I could not change the reality, I could begin to look for meaning in it. Once I was willing to look, finding became possible. I began, once again, to see life as evidence contrary to the concept of futility.

The great anthropologist Margaret Mead once lamented that Americans think every problem is solvable, so we never accept things as they are. Perhaps that is true. But when I met women in Africa who thought abuse in their marriages was acceptable or that suffering without medications was "just how things had to be," I soon found that I was fighting that sort of acceptance, in keeping with the rest of Niebuhr's prayer: ". . . the courage to change the things I can, and the wisdom to know the difference." It occurred to me that acceptance was necessary, but it wasn't enough. What I needed was wisdom, and another dose of courage.

The authors of a marvelous book, *The Spirituality of Imperfection*, make this bold assertion:

> *Spirituality is, above all, a way of life. We don't just think about it or feel it or sense it around us— we live it. Spirituality permeates to the very core of our human be-ing, affecting the way we perceive the world around us, the way we feel about that world, and the choice we make based on our perceptions and sensations. In the experience of spirituality, three essential elements are always at play: what we* see*; how we* feel*; and why we* choose.

In all things

I BELIEVE

there

is

meaning.

In very tangible ways, my spirituality has turned the relationship between my feelings and my behaviors upside down. For the first half of my life, I thought I acted in certain ways because of my feelings: I felt lonely, so I reached out for a man to comfort me. I felt overweight, so I would diet. My feelings produced my behaviors. My spirituality has taught me to reverse this: What I do can change what I feel. If I believe that all the significant things entering my life bring meaning, and that the ultimate meaning is love, then I can seek to use whatever has come my way to shape my loving acts. When I do, I feel healing as it occurs. It's like living life upside down.

The fact that I would die did not change the reality of each day that I was alive. Today, my children were near me and they were well. Today, I loved and was loved. That was the reality of my days, and when I could act as if my AIDS had brought a purpose, my spirituality kicked in. I could see AIDS as the source of dying and hatred, and so I could oppose it; I could *feel* dying with all its emotional and physical pain, and so I could speak powerfully of it; I could *choose* to use my life as a gift that I received whenever I gave it away.

I can look back on my life experiences—not just what's happened to me, but *what I've done with it*—and see that the moments of sharpest pain were also, in important respects, moments in which I was most aware of meaning, most immersed in serenity. It made sense to me when the authors of *The Spirituality of Imperfection* wrote:

> *Our very imperfections—what religion labels our "sins," what therapy calls our "sickness," what philosophy terms our "errors"—are precisely what bring us closer to the reality that no matter how hard we try to deny it, we are not the ones in control here. And this realization, inevitably and joyously, brings us closer to "God."*
>
> *One of the disconcerting—and delightful—teachings of [thirteenth-century philosopher and mystic Meister Eckhart] was: "God is closer to sinners than to saints." This is how he explained it: "God in heaven holds each person by a string. When you sin, you cut the string. Then God ties it up again, making a knot—and thereby bringing you a little closer to him. Again and again your sins cut the string—and with each further knot God keeps drawing you closer and closer."*

I'm cautious with the word *sin*. I do not imagine God sitting in heaven, pulling on strings. But replace the idea of *sin* with the reality of *pain*, and I'm all in—this explanation for growing toward a Higher Power makes perfect sense to me. I've been comforted because of the pain. It's the knots, not the string, that have enabled me to live with hope.

SPIRITUALITY IS SOMETHING WE all have, whether we acknowledge it or not. It's like health: good or bad, we have it. If I say I am "becoming more spiritual," what I probably mean—if I think about it—is that I am becoming more aware of my own spirituality. It was there all along, but for whatever reasons, I had not paid attention to it.

A few years ago, the pastor who'd first invited me to preach in his Presbyterian church on the East Coast invited me again, this time to the parish in Dallas, Texas, where he had resettled. He heard me trot out Mark Twain's puppy again. It worked as well in 2009 as it had in 1992. And he listened with his congregation while I looked back on my early days with AIDS as a time in which I was discovering meaning, not just living with a death sentence.

> *Initially, I heard and saw nothing of God's call in my AIDS. "Dying is an art, like everything else,"* wrote Sylvia Plath in her great poem, Lady Lazarus. *"I do it exceptionally well . . . I guess you could say I've a call." In accepting the idea that AIDS had not found me in some willy-nilly, meaningless accident, but that the virus had come to me for a purpose, I began to hear and respond to God's call in my life.*

I'd begun my career with AIDS begging God to take it away: *Please don't let me die. Please don't make my children into orphans.* The fact that ARVs came out of the laboratory years later, and have extended the lives of those who are able to use them, does not change the reality we discovered in those early years: I was dying. We all were dying. But what *did* change the reality of those early years was my eventual willingness to stop clinging to life as if my life depended on it.

Ironic? Paradoxical? Reality upside down? Sure. I found meaning, purpose, joy when I let go of trying to cling. You may know the old story:

> *George leaned too hard against the railing at the top of the Grand Canyon. It broke, and he plunged into the space below. Hurling down, flailing around, he crashed into a bush growing out of the canyon wall and was able to grab, hold on, and cling to his life.*
>
> *He'd been alone at the top, and now he was alone midway to the bottom. No one above could hear his screams; nothing lay below but death on the rocky canyon floor. Desperate, he cried, "God, help me!"*
>
> *As his cries echoed off the cliffs, he heard another voice. "All right," said God. George knew his rescue was at hand, and just as he began to offer thanks, God said, "Let go."*

George looked down at his certain death, then up at the heavens, and said, "God, you don't get it! I can't let go. It'll kill me!"

After a moment, God's response came back: "Let go."

Silence. Then a very soft voice, George's, could be heard to ask, "Is there anybody else up there?"

The story may be silly, but the point is rock-solid: When we are clinging to something with all our will, we are bound. Only when we let go—of addiction, obsession, self-pity, fear—can we experience freedom and usefulness.

When I had thought of my infection with AIDS only as a death sentence, the future looked bleak; when I saw it as the price of admission to a valuable AIDS community, things brightened a bit. Gradually, I began to accept the possibility that my AIDS wasn't a curse so much as a call. Maybe it was what qualified me to speak out on behalf of those who had less power, less protection, and fewer resources. I could afford to speak against the stigma and discrimination; I had financial means, insurance, healthy children, and the occasional bully pulpit. I could mount the stage in Houston and say, truthfully, that I was "one with" the dying infant and the struggling gay man. My raging against stigma and discrimination is possible because I am "one of them" on both sides of the dividing line: I live in a comfortable home in a comfortable community, doing comfortable things. I spoke to the Republicans saying "we," not "you": "We may take refuge in our stereotypes, but we cannot hide there long." But I could also speak for the AIDS community, for that other "we," when I stood on pulpits or mounted other stages. I could integrate messages from life on the road to AIDS into my art. I could author books, do interviews, give testimony. I could act on my spiritual conviction that I was called to do these things. When I acted, I felt better. Acting was healing.

When I stopped clinging to the self-pity of *Woe is me*, I soon discovered that there was an entire class of heroes on the road to AIDS. They were parents, siblings, nurses, hospice workers, physicians, aides, counselors, and strangers. They were *caregivers*—the generic term for people who do for us what we can no longer do for ourselves. Our nonprofit organization (the Family AIDS Network, which was active between 1992 and 2000) saw them and lifted them up for public awareness. For years, most had labored out of sight and without tribute; there were literally thousands of them doing heroic and unheralded work. Then we did a book as a tribute to them, *Angels in Our Midst: A Journal of Caregiving in Photographs and Words*. The tone of the book was set in its introduction:

> *If you've measured your own mortality, you've encountered some hard and doubting questions: Who will be there at the end, especially if it comes slowly? Who will demand that our pain be lessened, or soothe our lips with ice? Who will shepherd us through our terrors? Who will be patient with us, and treat us to the dignity we have lost? Sooner or later, a caregiver will be needed by each of us either to answer our hardest questions—or to tell us the answers don't really matter.*

My spirituality had matured—not to the state of perfection, but it was showing real progress. My mind and body were struggling to keep up with my soul. It was one thing to know you were called and that your life has meaning. What I was discovering is that it's something else to care.

THE EMPHASIS ON A spiritual life as a continual process of tangible experiences is important to me. Spirituality is within life, a part of life, a way to see things differently—an understanding that what appears to be ABC could be XYZ instead, that things may be upside down. My spirituality isn't about a certain dogma, because I don't have one. What I have is a story that, when I can tell it truthfully, shows my spirit growing, sometimes suddenly and sometimes gradually.

"It's all about love," Brian Weiss used to say as we'd wrap up one of our conversations. "Love resolves everything," says the man some call John of God. Neither of them is thinking about Hollywood romance. They have in mind the gritty, difficult, sometimes dangerous act of giving ourselves to others, of caring more deeply for a stranger than for myself, of loving whether or not I am loved in return. Glands and hormones won't produce this kind of love. Anthropologists may argue that we as a species are all about self-preservation, that our instincts are all about keeping ourselves alive. The spirituality I have come to embrace, however, says we reach our greater potential when we look outside of and beyond preserving the self. My spirituality says life will be good when I can let go of self, when I can give of myself to others. From the anthropologist's perspective, this may be upside down. Plus, it requires courage—sometimes more courage than I can summon. But it seems right to me.

Our actual spirituality is found in our actual behavior. Letting go of our self is a spiritual behavior and, even (or especially) when we are hanging above the rocks, the key to freedom. It seems contradictory and upside down, but it works. It explains why the most spiritual moment of my life was when I held the hand of the man who'd infected me with AIDS as he died, and I leaned in to whisper in his ear, "I love you." It took a lot of work for me to get there, but I learned just in time how much of our spirituality lives in the actions we choose.

If we don't put our spirituality into action and it gets divorced from our everyday behaviors, then we risk losing sight of the moral and ethical bedrock our lives demand. Does my worry strike you as overblown or absurd? Then come with me to a lynching being held somewhere on a dark Southern road. The womenfolk are laying out lunch, the menfolk are stringing up the rope, and everyone pauses for prayer before they hang the innocent man and set his lifeless body ablaze to shouts of "Praise God!" and "Hallelujah!" Our spirituality needs to link our spirit to the true Spirit of God, and when our spirit is truly anchored in God, it will be loving.

If my use of the god-language is off-putting for you, change it to the lingo that you are comfortable with—replace the word *God* with *the All* or *the Universe* or *the Mother* or whatever works for you. And if my illustration of a lynching with holy praise troubles you, change the example to . . . well, how about German hymns being sung as they kicked slow-moving, hungry children into the showers at Dachau?

Niebuhr's so-called Serenity Prayer became part of AA in the late 1940s and never left. Earlier, Bill Wilson had penned a prayer that now hangs on the walls of many twelve step meeting rooms. Its opening lines are, for me, the essence of sound spirituality: "God, I offer myself to thee, to build with me and to do with me as Thou wilt. Relieve me of the bondage of Self that I may better do Thy will."

AIDS is rotten. Cancer sucks. But if I can see life upside down, these illnesses can become gifts—gifts that I hate but for which I may yet be grateful. I can let go of my self to speak truth to power or whisper hope to the dying. When I do, self-pity evaporates and I can grasp a deeper meaning, and my joy in that moment is nearly perfect.

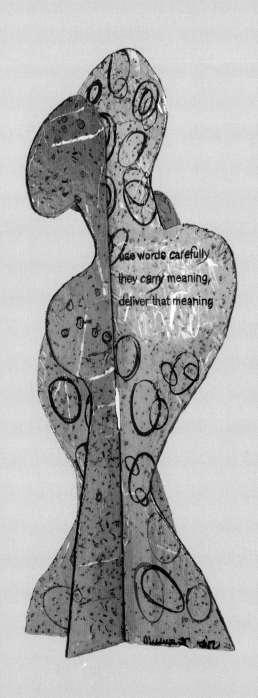

12

It's Just Fear

─────── SOUL OF HEART ───────

My body's soul has grown weary. My heart
is joyfully eager to serve, but my body's soul
cannot keep pace. My heart reassures me.
"We can go again, speak again, laugh and
sing and dance again." My soul says, "No, let
me stop and rest in silence." I love my heart's
enthusiasm. I think I will do this: give my soul
to my heart. When my soul belongs to my
heart, it will soar again.

─────────────────────────────

MOST AMERICANS HAVE NEVER heard of Larry Buendorf. He would prefer it stay that way. But Larry taught me perhaps the greatest lesson in my life. He showed me that courage is not the absence of fear but the willingness to do the right thing even though we're terrified.

Of all the Secret Service agents I met while serving in the White House Advance Office, Buendorf was the funniest. David Carpenter was a model of consistency. Skip Williams (his real name is Ashley, and he won't like my mentioning that either) guarded President Ford with a gentle protectiveness that I've never forgotten. Watching Skip quietly step forward when he didn't like what he saw in the crowd—always putting himself between danger and the president, never wanting to be noticed, never taking credit for courage—and seeing what all these men did for their country (not "for a living")—can still move me to tears.

Buendorf was the agent who could, at the strangest and least expected moments, make us all laugh. I remember being on the way to an important event with the president, and Buendorf had us all laughing hard. I asked him to stop because I could hardly breathe and I thought I was going to wet myself. The suggestion that I might lose bladder control amused him greatly, and he kept right on going. I didn't embarrass myself, no thanks to Buendorf.

On September 5, 1975, Lynette Fromme—a follower of mass killer Charles Manson, known as "Squeaky" because of her pinched, tinny voice—loaded a .45-caliber pistol, put on a nunlike robe, and became part of the crowd greeting President Ford in Sacramento, California. By the time Buendorf spotted her, she already had the gun in her hand and was swinging it in the direction of the president. In less than a second, literally less than a second, Buendorf chose not to shoot Fromme, because she was surrounded by waving adults and laughing children. As she raised her pistol, Buendorf plunged headlong into the crowd, rose directly into her line of fire, and snared her hand as she began to pull the trigger. Had the gun gone off, he would have taken the bullet.

When the chaos was over, Buendorf reappeared. He'd been making sure the president was safely removed, but he'd also been avoiding the media. When reporters spotted him, there was a scrum rush toward him. He ducked, turned, and promptly refused all interviews. When I asked him why, he muttered that he didn't want anyone to think that he'd been "heroic or anything."

Even months later, Buendorf hated discussing the incident. Asked what he was feeling when he plunged into the crowd, he'd shrug his shoulders. He'd go silent, or head for coffee, or come up with some ridiculous line that made us all laugh. But during late-night flights back to Washington, DC, in conversations held during back-of-the-plane poker games, agents would occasionally admit that fear is real.

In my earliest days of working at the White House, traveling with these guys (they were all men at that time) to advance a trip or accompany the president, I believed they didn't know fear. But I learned that I was wrong. "It's just fear," I remember one agent saying when I was once pestering them, "just fear . . ."

They didn't deny the fear; that wouldn't have worked. Instead, they denied fear the power to paralyze. Skip got between the president and danger. Buendorf got into the line of fire as Squeaky's finger began to tighten on the trigger. These guys knew fear, and they knew how they were going to act *anyway*. Fear? Sure. Paralysis? Absolutely not.

THE LESSON I LEARNED at the White House about fear was largely squandered during the months immediately following my HIV diagnosis. It wasn't quite *You name it and I'm afraid of it*, but that's not far off the mark. Those were nauseatingly terrifying days. Fear had power and took hold, and I did not know, could not remember, that it was "just fear." I suffered it, endured it, wept over it, felt paralyzed by it. It took five, maybe six months, with serious help from Brian Weiss and others, to get me back to the point where I realized that I was feeling fine—it was *just fear*.

Some folks say fear is a good instructor. I'm a skeptic. When we use harsh words or graphic explanations to teach our children not to run into traffic or put their hands on a hot stove, we may say we're using fear to teach, but I think a better term is *respect*. I didn't really want Max to be afraid of cars or traffic; I wanted him to respect the traffic's ability to harm him. Zack wouldn't be helped by being frightened of the stove; he just needed to respect the stove's ability to burn him.

Slavers taught obedience by branding and whipping, by selling slaves' sons and raping their daughters. Such brutality doesn't strike me as "teaching." That type of brutality is evil, not instructive. The same goes for those who traffic women and children for sex or cheap labor today. They don't "teach" their victims by spreading fear; they enslave them. Even using a milder version of fear, such as humiliating a child whose homework was forgotten or embarrassing a child who whispers to a classmate, strikes me as a sad strategy. In general, I think fear is a poor teacher.

Mostly, I think of fear as an enemy. My fear of telling my family and others about my diagnosis did nothing to improve how I told them, much less what I had to tell; it just added a lot of sleepless nights, useless terror, and tears. What I needed to do was come to a genuine understanding that what I was feeling was just fear. That's all. Once I could face that fear, I could act as if I were freed of it—because the power of fear had been diluted.

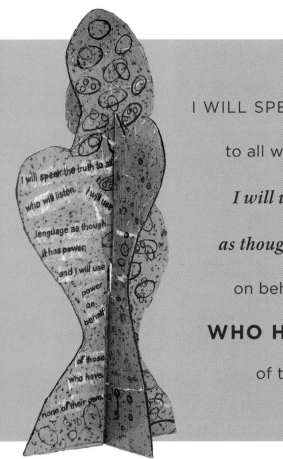

I WILL SPEAK THE TRUTH

to all who will listen,

I will use language

as though it has power

on behalf of those

WHO HAVE NONE

of their own.

As my sons grew older, I learned the fears that come with mother-hood, mostly variations on the theme of *I'll lose my children*. Early on, I feared losing them to accidents or illness. When they reached adolescence, I feared losing them to homicide (which I would commit if they continued all those disagreeable adolescent behaviors). As they became adults, these also proved to be "just fears." They avoided death, and I avoided prison.

The fear that I would be excluded from polite society because of my AIDS has never left me completely, because incidents pop up now and again to keep that fear alive. But I've done pretty well in recognizing when I am experiencing this familiar fear, and now I know how to manage it. Often, sensing the fear, I'm able to translate it into legitimate anger—for example, when first China and then Russia denied me a visa because of my HIV status. I may as well admit my parallel fear of being excluded from the AIDS community, which still consists mainly of gay men, because I'm a woman with children who was infected in her marriage. These fears are, at most, exaggerated.

My two most resilient fears have deep roots and probably border on neuroses. One is the fear of economic insecurity, which I experience despite the fact that I have more than I could possibly need in one lifetime. The other is the fear that I'll somehow lose my freedom to make choices; this hit a tender spot when AIDS dropped into my reality and I saw a future of declining health followed by the need for others to take over. Such deep-seated fears are what Bill Wilson called "soul-sickness." They are parasites that attach to our spirits and siphon our joy. The more we allow them to feed on us, the larger they become. They keep us alert as we dredge up evidence that the fears are right, that the disaster *du jour* really will happen this time. They are False Evidence Appearing Real (F.E.A.R.). These fears may be childhood's bogeymen, but they are bogeymen that can pursue us far into adulthood.

Sickness, incompetence, death, failure, poverty, rejection, shame—when I tell my story truthfully, these bogeymen become characters that help shape the plot. I can feel them viscerally, and I know that I've spent untold hours worrying about what has never happened and never will. But over time and through experience, as I've begun to identify them for what they are (just fears), their power has diminished.

When told that I had cancer, I experienced a moment of fear. But it was so unconvincing that it was only that one moment. Almost immediately, I thought of my cancer as irritating, inconvenient, a hassle. It was more frustrating than frightening. I was in a much more spiritually centered place than I was when I learned I had AIDS. I was older. Oh, and there's also this: Cancer is curable.

But the really big difference is that no one hates you because you have cancer. When I learned I had AIDS, I looked for a hiding place. When I learned I had cancer, I looked for a surgeon. Over time, I have learned that I can come out of the hiding place because my jailer is "just fear," not AIDS. But cancer came without any judgment or self-imposed sentence. I asked everyone who might know a good doctor to speak up.

I'm convinced that fear's greatest ally is silence. Silence is the environment in which fear thrives. The child who is being visited in the night by an abusive father will endure both the fear and the abuse, so long as silence reigns. The cowardly pimp, the predatory coach, the corrupt boss, the playground bully—their brutalities are protected, even encouraged, by silence. When we sense something that cannot be confessed or discussed, that is too big or too awful or too terrifying to admit, we are dealing with more than fear. We are dealing with silence, the protector of what is impermissible. It is still "just fear" at work, but we can't see it as such. We hear only the silence, see only the terror.

WITHIN A YEAR OF my diagnosis with AIDS, I knew that fear was the enemy and silence was giving it free rein. Scientists would be the ones to combat the virus, but advocates were needed to take on the twin enemies of fear and silence. I'm not sure whom I should credit with this recognition, although I tend to think that Brian Weiss was in on it. In any event, I went to Houston in 1992 armed with a speech that took on both fear and silence, beginning with the title: "A Whisper of AIDS."

The first third of the speech described the AIDS epidemic; the next third described America's response, including the reminder that "we cannot love justice and ignore prejudice, love our children and fear to teach them." But the final third—the "appeal"—was dominated by my belief that fear was the root cause of stigma, and silence was its best friend.

The entire speech consumed twenty-three written paragraphs. If I had numbered the paragraphs, I would have reached number 15 when I started to talk about the fear. I described the support my family had given me, then added, "But not all of you have been so blessed. You are HIV-positive but dare not say it. You have lost loved ones, but you dared not whisper the word *AIDS*. You weep silently; you grieve alone." I was speaking to the fear.

Paragraph number 16 also addresses fear: "I have a message for you: It is not you who should feel shame; it is we—we who tolerate ignorance and practice prejudice, we who have taught you to fear."

The lesson about fear, from paragraph number 18, has been requoted often: "I do not want [my children] to think, as I once did, that courage is the absence of fear; I want them to know that courage is the strength to act wisely when most we are afraid."

And my closing appeal went directly to fear and silence (paragraphs number 19 and 22): "To the millions of you who are grieving, who are frightened, who have suffered the ravages of AIDS firsthand: Have courage and you will find support . . . To all within the sound of my voice, I appeal: Learn with me the lessons of history and of grace, so my children will not be afraid to say the word *AIDS* when I am gone."

On the steamy night in Houston when I spoke, I actually believed if we could all see that prejudice and stigma were based on nothing but fear, and that such fear was groundless, the course of AIDS in America could be changed. I was convinced because I had seen fear up close and I knew it did not have to dominate us. I had learned that it's "just fear."

FRANKLIN D. ROOSEVELT'S FIRST inaugural address famously contained a line written four hundred years earlier by Francis Bacon: "We have nothing to fear but fear itself." Later in his inaugural, Roosevelt spoke to the power of the fear that had been set loose in America, a "nameless, unreasoning, unjustified terror which paralyzes." Perhaps it's unfair of me to apply Roosevelt's words to the political rhetoric that litters our airwaves and communities, but they seem to fit the bill.

The language and tenor of talk radio "commentary" today is brutal, angry, and suspicious; it spews fear. Radio hosts do not differ with the president; they find him "treasonous." Candidates do not claim different territory and then respectfully debate one another; instead, they engage in hostilities to win another vote or two. They use strategies and language designed for war; they mount attack ads designed to destroy. Selfishness masquerades as "true Americanism" when we're told that our taxes will never be raised because, after all, "those people" don't deserve our aid, our money, our partnership—"those people" being a reference to immigrants, the homeless, those who suffer illness or ignorance, all the people we're told we should fear, as if they are trying to take something from us. The Statue of Liberty's great "Give me your tired, your poor, your huddled masses" is far removed from the obscenities of today's rhetoric, so far removed from the statue's ideal that perhaps some illustrator should show the grand dame bending over and weeping. The rhetoric is persistent and noisy; its fuel is fear, and the fear is a "nameless, unreasoning, unjustified terror which paralyzes."

What I long for is a leader who moves beyond scare tactics, who champions decency, who calls us to our better instincts rather than appealing to our worst, who does not resort to fear-based tactics in the hope of scratching out a few votes. I remain as convinced that it is possible today as I was in Houston twenty years ago.

When someone steps forward to offer comfort and guidance based on respect, compassion, and love, that person will not need attack ads because the public's reverence for him or her will be palpable. Call me to a foreign policy based on global need, not instinctive fear, and we may find that winning the hearts and minds of others does not require billions of dollars for missiles and drones. Call me naïve, but I've seen the power of love and loyalty to overcome fear, and it ran toward the loaded gun, not away from it.

IN MARCH 1997 I was in Grand Rapids, Michigan, at the Gerald R. Ford Presidential Library and Museum, to open an exhibit of my *MESSAGES* collection. I keynoted an evening reception and spoke about the fear that had traveled down the road to AIDS with every one of the pilgrims. I told them of my freedom from fear, not because I was courageous but because I could afford medications and treatment. I spoke

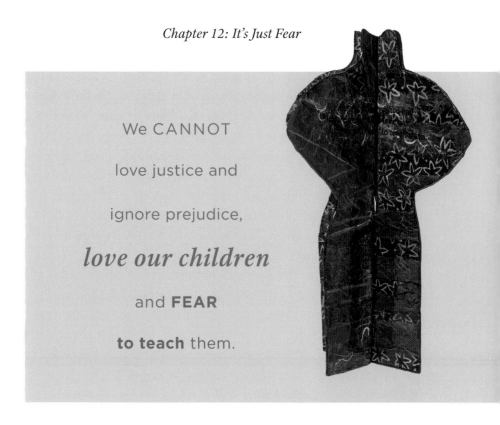

We CANNOT

love justice and

ignore prejudice,

love our children

and **FEAR**

to teach them.

of my own feelings of guilt, knowing that millions were hostages to the virus because they had no resources with which to fight. And I asked that the audience not walk away from these hostages, leaving them to die as if they did not matter.

I was honored to be in the place where the story of "my president" was told, including Buendorf's actions when Squeaky Fromme raised her gun. But I also had in mind an incident that was in the news shortly before I was scheduled to speak. Just before the 1996 winter holidays, a guerrilla band had gathered up hostages in Lima, Peru, moved them to an ambassador's well-fortified residence, and threatened to kill them all if demands were not met. The standoff went on for three weeks. After protracted negotiations, it was finally agreed that 225 of the nearly three hundred hostages would be set free.

The hostages themselves were isolated from all outside news and had no idea that most of them could soon know freedom. So when the guer-rillas began picking people, one by one, and leading them from the main rooms, hostages assumed that those chosen were slated to die. Among those who volunteered to go was a sixty-four-year-old priest, Father Juan

Julio Wicht, who had already won the hearts of the hostages: He had ministered to them all with a generous spirit, whether or not they shared his faith. He had given his food to those who were hungry, his bed to a man who had only the kitchen floor, comfort to all who were terrified.

As prisoners were chosen, grabbed, and removed, those being left behind were abused by the guards. Some were slashed, some beaten; all were shoved to the ground, sprawled out and vulnerable to the kicks that soon followed. They huddled in corners on cold floors, wishing for protection that did not come, hearing their tormentors' instructions to neither look up nor move, or they would be shot.

Father Wicht was at the doorway and nearly free when, seeing the welcoming crowd outside, he realized he'd volunteered for freedom, not death. In the hallway shadows, with a pistol at his head, he paused, turned back, and refused to be pushed through the door into the sunlight. For a moment, the man of God spoke with anger. "I will walk out the door," he growled at his captors, "with the last hostage to be freed."

The man chosen to take Father Wicht's place became the 225th prisoner to be released that day. When asked what he saw as he was being ushered out, he said it was "a miraculous thing": When Father Wicht had walked back into the holding area, every hostage—the old, the sick, the broken—had struggled to rise. At risk of death, the witness said, every prisoner stood to greet Father Wicht with an ovation the shocked guards could not prevent. Fear was mighty, but it could not hold a candle to love. "The last thing I saw," said prisoner number 225, "was all of them standing. The last thing I heard was their applause."

The power that fear holds over us is broken the moment we deny it, the moment we say no to it, the moment we squash it with compassion, love, and caring. This may seem upside down to those who draft the attack ads, but my experience tells me that we will be conquerors only when we give up seeking to conquer. This upside-down concept works; it really does.

On that grim day in Peru, with every good reason to feel bone-chilling terror, the weak and imprisoned rose up and cheered. When they stopped clinging to what they feared losing, they were as free as the 225 who had been physically freed.

This isn't some kind of woo-woo, other-worldly, goofy religious stuff. It's gritty, tough, hard reality in a world where torture thrives and murder often seems to win. I'm telling you, the guys at the back of the plane were right: It's "just fear." And that simple Brazilian rancher is right, too: Love resolves everything.

13

Breaking

PLAYFUL SOUL

Once—far, far away—my soul was light and whimsical. I remember having a playful soul as a child. And, later, when my children were very young; I was playful then. I remember it as an uncertain echo, through a mist that lays over these years "before . . .": before diagnosis, before the plague, before the dying and the medications and the incredible weariness. I think my soul was playing once. I think . . .

"WHEN I WAS CONFIRMED at Temple Beth El, the one thing I knew was that I could never again be a stranger." It was December 1, 2000, the millennial World AIDS Day, and I was back at Beth El, on the outskirts of Detroit, speaking to my home congregation. I remembered my 1963 confirmation, my confidence that I was "a member in full, a child of the covenant, a woman whose place in her tradition was unmovable. I would always be able to claim my identity, always be able to claim my community, always have a sense of belonging. I could never again be a stranger."

Such hopeful imaginings are appropriate to a fifteen-year-old, coming of age and surrounded by smiling, approving adults. By the year 2000 I had passed my fiftieth birthday. Over the intervening thirty-seven years, I'd carried a pervasive sense that I was a survivor. *No matter what happens to me*, I thought, *I will somehow get through it.* I am strong. But by the time I returned to Temple Beth El, that sense of invincibility had taken more than a few lumps.

A major challenge to my optimism was life inside the American world of AIDS. I joined that world technically, by diagnosis, in 1991, and publicly in 1992. What I began to recognize early on was that people with AIDS had little to hang onto except hope. Nothing else was available. We were, individually and collectively, a band of viral hostages being rounded up for the final kill. Some had earlier appointments with death and some had later engagements, but we all had an expiration date, and we all knew it. We clung to the hopeful idea that there had to be purpose in the plague and therefore in our lives. Most of us secretly harbored the idea that perhaps we would miraculously slip through death's grip. We tracked reports on "long-term survivors," those who'd lived for more than ten years since their diagnosis. We read every rumor that someone had been cured—usually someone vaguely described and living in a foreign country; like all good rumors, they were neither proven nor debunked. We wanted to believe the National Institutes of Health, the Centers for Disease Control, the major pharmaceutical firms, and even the off-the-wall upstart companies chasing exotic notions, all of which claimed to see light at the end of the tunnel. Their annual reports were full of it. Those of us living with the virus didn't see the light, although we knew all about groping in the tunnel. "Hope is tenacious," Paul Laurence Dunbar once wrote. "It goes on living and working when science has dealt it what should be its death-blow." In the chill of that dark tunnel, we kept looking for light.

It took me a few years to conclude, sadly, that, if science was not going to rescue us, politics wouldn't do the job either. My experience immediately after the 1992 Republican National Convention in Houston had lifted my hopes for real government intervention. Senators and cabinet secretaries were only too happy to take my calls. The president wanted me on the National Commission on AIDS. The media covered every appeal made by the AIDS community. But that was 1992. At the 1996 Republican convention, I was booked as the adult in what both Papaharry and Johnny Carson would have called "a kid act." It was downhill from there. As the new millennium approached, I felt like a blip on yesterday's radar screen. By the late 1990s, practically everyone with the disease—two generations of gay men and nearly every acute hemophiliac in America—had died. The road to AIDS was lined with graves, one long cemetery.

My sense of growing uselessness to my fellows with AIDS was becoming palpable. On World AIDS Day 1998, I flew to North Carolina to keynote ceremonies hosted by the giant pharmaceutical Glaxo Wellcome. The company had poured untold millions of dollars into HIV/AIDS research and more on drug development and marketing. Early antiretroviral combinations (ARVs), a constantly shifting "cocktail" of drugs—were already being prescribed to qualifying American patients, including me. I expressed gratitude early in my remarks and then made what I termed "an immodest proposal":

> *My proposal is that Glaxo Wellcome leave us to die of AIDS. . . . If Glaxo Wellcome withdrew from the field, that would be a story. Just outline the case to the media. Tell them, "There's no market here. No one really cares about these people except us. We're going to lose money and lose stockholders. It's a bad investment, so we're going to step aside. And if they die, they die."*

Suggesting that Glaxo Wellcome take a powder on AIDS, even with tongue firmly in cheek, was a somewhat gloomy solution. But the dominant mood was grim among those of us with the virus. We longed for one major headline telling the world that AIDS was here, that it was killing us, that someone cared. Behind this wish lay the latent uncertainty about a pharmaceutical fix. Having overdosed on high expectations when AZT was introduced a decade earlier, the AIDS community was collectively leery.

What was true of the AIDS community in general was doubly true for women living with AIDS. I'd lobbied private industry and government leaders, and always the arguments visited the same impasses: *Women don't have AIDS.*

Okay, they have AIDS but they don't want to participate in research studies.

Okay, they say they'll participate, but then they don't drive . . . don't speak English . . . don't have child care.

If I was still arguing by this time, there was always the kill shot: *Okay, but Mary, there's no money for research on women.* The result was that women were taking drugs developed by, with, and for men, because there was nothing else to take. It felt as though we didn't matter.

Beginning in early 1996, it became increasingly apparent that ARVs were likely prolonging the lives of people with AIDS, women as well as men. We kept waiting for the dying to commence again; it didn't happen. There was no obvious date when our outlook shifted—no moment before which the AIDS community was skeptical and after which we were convinced. But arguments of ARV failure were fading, and testimonies to ARV success were stacking up. As the evidence supporting the efficacy of ARVs mounted, I began to realize—vaguely at first, but with increasing certainty—that, as I told an audience some years later, I was "no more prepared in 1996 for the prospect of a long life than I had been in 1991 for the promise of a short one."

The changes ARVs produced within people I knew were often astounding. The "Lazarus effect" was real: Wasting bodies that had degenerated into skeletal outlines were suddenly filled out and strong. Thin, weedy voices turned robust again. Men and women who'd said their final goodbyes to friends now called to schedule lunch. Family, friends, and more than a few physicians began to expect that those who'd received a death sentence would now inhale the breath of life and take to dancing in the streets. But I wasn't in a dancing mood. I was in neutral, neither driving forward with hope nor backpedaling in fear. I was frozen somewhere in the middle, wondering whether Lazarus would be around long.

Uncertainty about whether ARVs were a permanent fix was only part of the ambiguity. I was amazed to discover that I was also reluctant to accept the news that I was not going to die. It wasn't merely a question of *Would the drugs work?* It was, astonishingly, *Do I want them to work?*

Of course I wanted to live. I loved my children and did not want to leave them. But I'd been planning for a graceful, if unhappy, early exit. I'd already told the world I was on my way out. I'd finished my estate plan. My story was supposed to end soon, on a note of loving self-sacrifice. I had pinned my hope on a legacy, not a long life. I was hoping to die well.

I imagine now that I felt a tinge of guilt at the prospect of living. I'd told the world that "my children will inevitably turn to orphans." Everyone was sorry. They applauded and they cried. Now what was I supposed to say—"Just kidding"?

1998 WAS A TUMULTUOUS year. Despite the ARVs, I was sick. By the time I arrived at the Glaxo Wellcome speech in December, in addition to my immodest proposal I had an announcement to make: I was going off ARVs. I would be taking my chances with the virus.

I was taking the so-called cocktail until days ago, when my physician and I concluded that the real side effects from the drugs were worse than the potential death from the virus. It was a tough decision, in part because we don't know where we'll head next. But the decision was only hard to make because it involves life and death. The evidence that drove the decision was plain and simple.

When the first bout of nausea and other symptoms struck, I comforted myself and amused others with the observation "Well, I won't have to diet during the holidays." But I'd been prematurely hopeful. Weight came as if from the air, and with it unexpected body changes ranging from bloating to fat deposits to assaults no self-respecting woman will admit.

Then came the restless sleep, the ten- and twelve- and fourteen-hour stretches in bed, only to rise exhausted, too tired to care for my children. When I moved, joints made loud noises. When I moved quickly, sharp pains exploded and dull aches followed each movement.

Without *courage*

we would

give up the battle.

Without *compassion*

the battle

has **no purpose.**

Blood tests said that T-cell counts were going up and viral loads were going down. Everyone said, "Isn't that great!" I nodded and went back to bed—hoping that someone would make sure Max's homework was done and Zack remembered to bring his bug collection to school in the morning.

In fact, as the viral load descended, so did I. If I was winning the battle against the virus, I was losing the fight to live. No amount of antidepressants could catch my cascading emotions—the loss of self-worth, the loss of confidence, eventually [the] loss of hope and desire to live.

Twice I remember being especially distressed. The first time was when my physician said he did not really know how to manage the side effects, because there'd not been adequate testing on women . . . The second time I became distressed was when I tried to explain to myself why I was doing this, why I was taking drugs that day after day made me sicker and sicker.

I want to live because I have children. It isn't about hanging on to life at any cost, or about imagining that I deserve to live more than others. I have a simple, elemental desire to see my sons grow up. I'd like to adjust Max's tie when he heads out for his first formal dance, cheer for Zack when he plays his first varsity game, cry in the audience if either of them should one day take a bride. My wishes are enormously ordinary. I want to watch my sons become adults.

But when your hours are spent rotating between bathroom and bedroom, there's no time to see that lunches are made and faces are washed. Dental appointments give way to bouts of nausea. Routine tasks become impossible. Life consists of alarm clocks and daily schedules wrapped around times to take pills and then times to be sick because of the pills.

Glaxo Wellcome has created miracle drugs; you really have. But drugs can't work every miracle that each of us pray for. They have limits. And they have drawbacks. And they have—oh, my, they really have—side effects.

My private decision was soon public news. The *Washington Post* published an Abigail Trafford commentary, "Treatment: At What Cost?" that described my choice. It opened:

She couldn't do it—couldn't keep taking the drugs that made her feel worse than the disease. It didn't make any sense to her. The drugs were not going to cure her; they were just going to buy her more time. But what kind of time? She says she didn't have a life while taking the drugs. The nausea and fatigue and all-over aching—like a bad case of the flu that never went away. She couldn't get out of bed, could barely speak on the phone.

By late February 1999, everyone who might have cared knew that I had stopped taking the cocktail. At the suggestion of my doctor, Mike Saag, I publicly described it as a "drug holiday," a term familiar in the world of AIDS since the mid-1980s. When toxins from prescribed drugs built up to near-lethal levels, AIDS patients would take some time off the drugs, allowing the virus to flourish for a while in exchange for lower levels of toxicity. Now it was my turn to be drug-free. I was "on holiday."

Stuart White, a friend since our days at Cranbrook, wrote a personal note both urging me to live and accepting my decision to feel well again: "I want to argue logically that your choice should be reconsidered, because I want to dance with you at some distant reunion. But far more importantly, you need to dance with Max and Zachary tomorrow and the next day and the next."

All told, I was off the ARVs for most of a year before the virus showed that it had gained the upper hand. As usual, Mike had a solution: He offered a new cocktail combination that would present limited side effects. Once again, Mike was able to blend his knowledge and the latest therapies to keep the virus at bay. But even the best prescribed drugs have side effects, and over the years Mike's best tools have brought my toughest challenges.

For a dozen years—roughly from 1998 to 2010—I felt life slowly spiraling downward in broad, unhappy cycles of problems, medications, sadness, exhaustion, loss of purpose, and depression. I didn't have any free-fall, leaden-weight drops where I woke up fine one day and suicidal the next. Neither was it a straight-line descent like an airplane on a long approach to landing. I cycled—sometimes slowly, sometimes quickly—but always I cycled.

The problems I faced were mostly ordinary: children becoming teenagers, my aging, relationships faltering. The medications I needed were potent, and it was difficult to know when a "symptom" (pain, weight gain, sleep loss, feeling "down") was a side effect and when it was simply life. Sadness followed some losses, especially my father's death. Every cycle increased the exhaustion—a tiredness so profound I cried at the thought of moving my legs to get out of bed. And when the exhaustion made it impossible to give speeches and do advocacy work, I felt less useful, less worthy, less necessary.

What sustained me during these years was a sense of hope, my conviction that life is worth living. I'd hear echoes of Brian Weiss urging me to listen to the voices and deliver messages of love. I'd focus on a piece of art or a collection, and feel momentarily inspired. Hope took a bruising, but it did not die.

Until 2009. Depression settled in like Gila Bend heat in July. Not only did I lose hope; I resented it. I convinced myself that I'd been used, a poster girl for Republicans and a lunch ticket for hangers-on. My art was dull. My spirituality was nothing more than childish imagination—and, speaking of children, mine would be better off without me. Had someone offered me Nietzsche's famous quote about hope—"Hope is the worst of all evils because it prolongs man's torments"—I'd have bought his book.

I had broken earlier cycles by taking a geographic cure. Spiraling down in 2001, I had moved from New York to Florida, ostensibly to take advantage of a special school that would meet the needs of my sons. At the time, my parents were there, my attorney was there, I had roots there, and I believed that if something should happen to me, Max and Zack would be cared for there.

In the late 1990s I'd begun going to Africa. Once there, I could feel my sense of purpose return, and with it came energy. The women's laughter was infectious. They wanted me to show them how to make jewelry that I could then sell, returning income to them. I visited Africa again and again—with the boys, with friends, with United States and UN officials, with my siblings and their families. I came home tired but energized, higher than I'd been when I left—but still lower than I'd been the last time I'd returned from Africa. Each year the cycle left me a bit worse off. The geographic cure had limitations.

By January 2010 my depression could not be masked. Mike and I argued about my medications. He believed I needed something newer and better, so he changed my cocktail again. I was convinced the growing depression was a side effect of the new combination; he said the odds of this were "less than 2 percent." Something needed to break the impasse.

I agreed to Mike's suggestion that I spend a week at Johns Hopkins in a special program to deal with my depression. One week stretched into a month-long *One Flew Over the Cuckoo's Nest* experience. Six months later, I had a return engagement—but the second time, I'd secured an agreement: We would deal not just with psychic pain but also with medication changes. By the time I left Johns

The

ANTIDOTE

to our

grief

is God's

grace.

Hopkins in late July 2010, my medications had been changed, the depression had lifted (I still believe it was a side effect), and the cycle had been broken. Life was worth living. I knew hope again. No need to sell the house and move.

HOPE HAS GARNERED MORE than its share of political attention recently. It's practically become a plank in the campaigns of the Democratic Party. Bill Clinton famously claimed in his 1996 convention acceptance speech that "I still believe in a place called Hope, a place called America." If Clinton believed in his hometown's name, his Democratic successor—President Barack Obama—raised that belief to new heights when he spoke powerfully at the 2004 convention, lifting up a vision of "hope in the face of difficulty, hope in the face of uncertainty—the audacity of hope!"

I think of hope less in political than in personal terms. It is a quiet friend, a deeply spiritual advisor. It tells me that even if my joints ache and the surgeon says, "It's cancer," life is worth soldiering on. In the serenity and calm of a spiritual retreat, I've sensed that life has purpose, that love defines the arc of history, and that my spirit and the Spirit of the Universe can flow together, commune together, sometimes dance together. I experience this loving flow, and the experience leaves me with hope.

"Hope is independent of the apparatus of logic," wrote author and activist Norman Cousins as he used Marx Brothers films and vitamin C to battle pain and illness. Hope doesn't rely on the evidence. It creates its own evidence by stirring me to action, getting me out of bed and out of myself and into life. Hope is an experience, not a theory; it's based on action, not just belief. I've experienced hope, and I've experienced its absence.

When I am in the midst of a first-rate funk, getting out of my self-centered universe and immersing myself in the lives of women in Africa has regularly brought me an experience of hope. Listening to my children talk about their career plans is an experience in hope. Living life on life's terms, with a sense of spirituality that is "upside down"—where my failings in the past qualify me as a healer of others in the future—is an experience in hope.

My discovery that fear is "just fear" has both staunched the loss of hope when I sense fear and fueled new hope when I realize I can act despite the fear. George Iles once wrote that "hope is faith holding out its hand in the dark." If you have ever heard a diagnosis of AIDS, or cancer, or clinical depression—or anything else that siphons joy and pumps in panic—you know the need to reach out into the dark. The problem, of course, is that you do not want to make the reach; you are paralyzed by the fear or the reality. You cannot move. Then hope quivers in your soul, and you reach out to someone you love, or you whisper, "Thank you," to the nurse bending over you in the night. Your body relaxes as your soul expands, and you experience hope.

When I'm allowed to carry all this into a sermon or speech; when I am able to inspire someone in the dim reaches of the room; when in the quiet afterward that person finds me and says, "I'd given up hope and you've restored it"—these are the moments when I experience the value of life and, therefore, the power of hope.

The cycle that led deep into depression is gone now, at least on hiatus. In fact, I think it's been permanently broken. I've been healed. Surely Mike's character and his medicine are a critical part of my healing. So is the quiet of my studio at dawn, and so is a note from a friend saying I've made a difference. I've experienced a spiritual healing, not a religious one, and a healing once experienced cannot be denied. Instead of hearing the dark voice within me speaking hopeless gibberish, I hear the resonant voice of the great Maya Angelou, looking up from her own grief and saying confidently, "God puts rainbows in the clouds so that each of us—in the dreariest and most dreaded moments—can see a possibility of hope." It makes me thankful for a God of hope.

14

Running After Happiness

The perfect couple stepped from their BMW and walked into my studio gracefully, elegantly. They looked through pieces while I cleaned tables, answered phones, moved furniture. "Do you work here?" I said, "Yes," and they asked if there were more quilts like the one she was touching. "It's a soul quilt," I said—but they heard "sole," not "soul," and headed for the door. I let them go. My "soul creation" was what they thought, one-of-a-kind. A moment of my soul.

THE IDEAL OF LOVING others without any expectation that they will love in return is much praised and seldom practiced, because it's hard. Who wants to love someone who won't love you back? "God" is the answer suggested by some religions. But I am not God. And loving this way, for me, is a stretch.

The first requirement of a selfless love is already apparent: being selfless. My self can be sad and want to be comforted, sick and want to be healed, frightened and want to be reassured—and if you love me, my self is inclined to think you'll want to do all the comforting, healing, and reassuring. What my self thinks, I soon expect. So it goes: I set out arranging a selfless love . . . and wind up loving with strings attached.

In addition to attaching strings to my love, I can easily think of love as an emotion, a feeling. This is harder territory for me, frankly, because I have felt love, have experienced the emotion. I've been held in the arms of a lover; I remember it. I can go back to the moment I first saw Max after his birth, first lifted Zack into my arms, and already I'm reliving feelings so intense that I have never tried describing them. Separating love and emotion is impossible.

Over time I've come to believe that this, too, is upside-down territory. Once I thought that the emotion of love would produce actions that were loving. Flowers arrive with a surprisingly romantic note. I'm told that I'm pretty when I feel like yesterday's coffee grounds. Someone loves me, and I know because this person is acting a certain way. But much more reliable is this formula: If I engage in loving actions, the feeling of deep satisfaction will result. Actions will produce emotions—it's upside down.

The ancient Greeks had it right. They had multiple words to describe what we try to jam into one. *Eros* was romantic love (think *erotic*), *philea* was familial love (as in Philadelphia, the City of Brotherly Love), and *agape* was unconditional love (love without expectation of return). Different words are helpful because, for example, to be "loving"—to engage in loving actions—may have no relationship at all to "being in love." When I am *in love,* I'm euphoric, drunk on hormones of happiness; it's an incredibly self-pleasing moment. When I strive to be *loving,* and I am asked for a dollar by a drunk who hasn't showered since defecating in his stained trousers, or when I'm led to a ranting schizophrenic who wants me drenched in her fury—these are not Romeo-and-Juliet moments. The emotions summoned by encounters with the drunk or the deranged tie more closely to revulsion than romance. No violins play as I struggle to act out of love instead of running away. Having words that accurately describe these differences could help avoid some of the confusion.

My experience with *being in love* has been mixed. In some moments I was too needy, and in others probably too giving. But I'm grateful to have known the experience and to have children as a living testimony to that experience.

My lessons in *acting lovingly* have come from less giddy spots. In Betty Ford, I saw how to give of oneself in acts of courageous service. She truly used what was bad in her life to bring good to the lives of others. Although I did not learn this lesson perfectly, I learned it memorably. I owe her more than I was able to tell her. From the treatment center, I took the possibility of seeing life upside down: By being unshackled from "the bondage of self," I found myself freed to care for others. Brian Weiss reinforced lessons saying, in effect, that when my actions aligned with the Divine Will, amazing things could happen. In fact, I did experience some of those amazing things.

The magazine *Marie Claire* invited me to speak at a New York luncheon in February 1996. The audience was mostly wealthy and female. I had been contending with my first significant bout of side effects and failing health and had been thinking long and hard about the meaning of life. During my speech, I was midway through a rant about failed United States policy on AIDS when, essentially out of nowhere, I dropped in the following:

> *It has taken me nearly fifty years, and one extraordinarily mean virus, to learn two basic truths. The first is that the value of our life is measured not by its length but by its depth. In my own case, AIDS may cost me some length but it has driven me to new depths. The other lesson is this: We don't find our life's purpose in ourselves. We find it in serving others. It's in spending ourselves on behalf of others that we become rich.*

In this speech, my tribute to the importance of serving others was brief. This conviction was continuing to emerge after years, as a child and a young adult, of being taught by my parents to "give back." Since perhaps the mid-1980s I've increasingly recognized the urgency of putting service at the core of my life if I want to be happy. The principle has gained momentum, starting as a small tremor and gradually becoming a life-changing tsunami. By the time I spoke for *Marie Claire*, I knew it to be true. Since then, I've experienced it over and over and over again.

Echoing the Prayer of St. Francis, I've learned—sometimes painfully—that I am most satisfied, most contented, most happy when I seek not to be served but to serve. Were life to be measured by the rules on television's "reality" shows, where winners are shrewd and self-serving, and humbler candidates get sent home, St. Francis would choose to go with the loser. My experience tells me that I'll be most grateful if I run to catch up to the saint and the loser. Let me go with them in an upside-down world, where the losers win.

I'VE ALWAYS BEEN SENSITIVE to the gap between rich and poor, but I've not always bridged that gap out of love. In my earliest years, it was difficult to distinguish between service for others that is motivated by love and "service" that is motivated instead by guilt—guilt at having more than others have, or more than I need, when they have less than they need. Often, I think, I was driven by guilt. And the problem with guilt is that it's essentially self-focused. When feeling guilty about myself in relation to others, I'm still focused on me: my errors, my bank account, my shortfalls, my selfishness. Guilt is always, ultimately, "all about me." Love, and true service, is not. But I wasn't always able to see the importance of this distinction.

When I began spending time in Africa, the economic and social gaps were so pronounced that "white guilt" was obvious; even I couldn't miss it. And having identified it, I was able also to watch it fade under a growing sense of truly loving service. What early on sent me to my hotel room burdened with feelings of guilt eventually gave way to loving actions, to finding ways I could genuinely serve those around me.

Africa changed my life. When I felt like a freak in what was supposed to be "my own world," I could go to Africa and be just another woman with AIDS among many women with AIDS. When we all got over the shock—they, of my whiteness; me, of their joy—we had a great time together. I taught them to make jewelry, and they taught me to be grateful.

Not everything is perfect in a world of poverty, disease, and instability. Hunger cannot be dressed up as virtuous. In Africa, as everywhere, corruption has its way. But my dominant experiences in Africa have been of people who are caring and generous. They return trust with trust, truth with truth. They have accepted me in ways I might neither have imagined nor deserved. Among the many lessons they've driven home for me is the need to live in the moment, to take each day as a gift, to be grateful for all I have, and to know that everything given to me is on loan, to be shared with others.

Giving of ourselves can be done in many ways, ranging from daily, incremental kindnesses to endowments. Some may "give all they have to the poor." Among Americans of wealth, philanthropy is an option that is increasingly chosen. I'm a fan of foundations that make up the bulk of American's philanthropic networks. The good that's been done through the legacy of Robert Wood Johnson and the foresighted giving of people like Bill and Melinda Gates is incalculable. Our family has a substantially less-endowed foundation, but even we have been able to contribute significant funds to an AIDS program in Zambia. That said, our grants have been gifts with strings. We expected some reporting, some accountability, some demonstration that the money would be used in the ways that had been proposed. We wanted to see outcomes. I've come to believe that donors may give money to philanthropies to serve others, but philanthropies give grants on the model of a financial transaction: *We'll give you this if you give us that.* It's philanthropy, not charity—good acts, but not necessarily loving actions.

201

If *philanthropy* is typically well-organized, systemic, planned, and published, much *charity* is at the opposite end of the giving spectrum, an accident of the heart: it just pours out when compassion is evoked. My sons have experienced rushes of compassion especially while in Africa. Max accompanied us on a recent trip, after he'd already found his calling as a filmmaker. Working on a documentary dealing with AIDS, he toiled from dawn to dusk most days, not because he hoped for an Academy Award but because he saw this as a place he could make a difference if his film truly captured needs that motivated Americans to act. He "got it." He understood that we are satisfied when we serve—and that we can't find true satisfaction when we don't.

Zack was nine or ten the first time he went with me to Africa. My notes, to which I gave the title "Our Africa Trip," ended on a discovery Zack had made: "What he learned wasn't always how someone lived in

Africa; it was what was inside them and how they loved and helped others." What Zack could admire was that people he'd met cared for one another. They did not know about philanthropy and foundations, but they demonstrated loving actions on a day-by-day, hour-by-hour basis. Zack did not feel guilty at having more; he felt admiration for what they had: love for one another. He "got it."

JENNIFER MOYER WAS ALREADY fighting the breast cancer that killed her when we were putting final touches on *Angels in Our Midst*, a book of photographs and text dealing with caregivers within the American AIDS epidemic. It was 1997. Jennifer, half of the publishing company Moyer Bell, had brought her laughter and brilliance to my life four years earlier as we published the first anthology of my speeches. She always referred to the new book on which we were working by the title's first word, and she lived long enough to see her *Angels* published.

The original idea of *Angels in Our Midst* was to make sure the world knew about the heroes who were caring for people with AIDS. The pioneer caretaker in my life was Patricia Gibbons, whom I had met in Boston during my husband Brian's illness. "Pat" Gibbons was, for me, the person who modeled caregiving. As I was getting to know Pat, I was beginning to see the depth, power, and grace that has emerged from the hospice movement over the last half a century.

I started taking cameras with me as I traveled to give speeches, and my skills behind any camera improved considerably after some mentoring by a friend from my time in the Ford White House: Pulitzer Prize–winning photographer David Kennerly. Once David understood what I was trying to do with the camera, he taught me how to use it as if it were an extension of my body. It was no more separated from me than my eyes; it was "me." At the same time I was taking lessons from David, some caregivers, and some of those for whom they were caring, began to take down barriers, allowing me into their most intimate moments. The idea of *Angels* was on its way to becoming a reality.

When I began to practice what David had preached, through the lens of my cameras I began to see more than objects in front of me. I saw relationships. I saw motivations. I saw, and tried to capture, love. I saw, at incredibly close range, again and again, how women and men brought comfort and healing to those who could not be made comfortable or healed. I saw service in ways, in actions, that I would have thought impossible. What I saw, I tried to photograph. Sometimes it worked.

When I was convinced we had enough material, both photographs and words, the tone of the book was set in the dedication: "To Michael Saag, physician, researcher, cousin, and caregiver, who taught me that science without love is lifeless, and that great healers never deny the grief—they are merely undefeated by it." *Undefeated* is an understatement. Great healers and caregivers "are so perfectly unselfconscious," I said in the foreword, "that they do not know their own staggering goodness."

> *Entering the room of someone wrestling with death is an act of invasion. These are intimate places shrouded with vulnerability and mystery. To come in carrying a camera seems sacrilegious . . . The overwhelming sense of these places is less of illness than of heroism displayed by those who've come not as chroniclers but as comforters: the father who held his stranger-son's hand as it grew cool . . . the grandmother who whispered away the fears of the grandson she adored . . . the doctor who loved, and did not leave, those he could not heal. Compassionate caregiving is almost beyond imagination, even after you've encountered it firsthand.*

Across America we had traveled, visiting hospices and prison cells, hospital wards and private homes. Some moments were simple, and simply staggering.

> *As if Rock's body had not suffered enough with AIDS, he'd also endured another round of chemotherapy. He was sick when we arrived. The room was dark. He told me how grateful he was for the support of his friend, Steve. They sat on the couch together and talked. But his eyes told me that his greatest caregiver—the one he trusts most, the one he fears someone will take from him before he dies—is Abby. "She's still a puppy," he said. Rock and Steve wanted a picture of me with Abby. I think I was crying.*

As we worked on *Angels*, we all experienced the power of stories being told to us, shown to us. I was living with AIDS, Jennifer was living with

WE who

are human

are,

all of US,

one.

cancer, and neither of us knew about our future. What we knew was our own increasing need for care—a need neither of us welcomed. And so we worked, page by page, story by story, unfolding these private memorials, tributes to love in action.

In Atlanta it was Alice, who looked the part of a country club matron, immaculately dressed and holding herself with an erect, almost formal bearing. When I first met Alice, I wondered if she could ever express an emotion. And then I went into her thirty-year-old son's room where I saw that, beyond all question, she "adored David. If he were childlike again—welcoming the stuffed animal she'd brought today—she was happy to be motherly, to care for her child. When she sat in a nearby chair, and he smiled, she beamed . . . caring for her man-child as he slipped away."

From New York's Rikers Island prison to the Rue's House shelter in Los Angeles, from West Palm Beach to Grand Rapids, I trailed caregivers. They'd come from hospices, congregations, families, hospital staffs, visiting nurse associations, and parts unknown. They never "acted the part," performing for me or the camera. Instead, they went about their daily and nightly routines of love-in-action, proving that love is a verb, offering a muscular love that gives without hope of return.

I now find myself wondering what Jennifer was thinking when she edited a few of the paragraphs. Her own cancer was intense, and treatments were grueling. Like me, she had small children. What I know is that she, too, saw the book—her *Angels*—as service, as an opportunity to use her mother's heart and editorial skills to give something important to others. Some of what the angels gave us, so we could give to others, was tough.

Dying is not pretty and rarely graceful. Only on Hollywood sets is it clean and odorless. If we die slowly enough to have others care for us near the end, it's a physical struggle that involves a mean betrayal by our own bodies. First we lose control, then we lose dignity, then we lose life, more or less in that order.

The extraordinary power of the caregivers I've met is in the ways they find to give back what our bodies take from us. They see to it, in amazingly detailed and tangible ways, that the person whose hours are numbered stays in charge of painkillers, of color schemes and music choices, of who comes and who's barred from coming. When the coughing spells lead to spurts of vomit, when bowels and bladders empty without warning, caregivers are neither surprised nor offended. I've heard them say, with quiet grace and good cheer: "I'm so glad you got that out; you'll feel better now." Love is not sanitized in this setting. It is gritty, unquestioned, and spectacular.

And it is about as far removed from hormonal romance as life will take us.

I've never tried to count the ways or the number of hours that I've chased happiness in my life. Especially in my younger years, I looked and tried almost anything that seemed as though it would lift the weight of uncertainty or unhappiness and make me joyful. I kept thinking I could find it in another glass of wine, another relationship, another job, another city. And so I chased, sometimes to the point of exhaustion, certain that it—happiness—must be out there somewhere, waiting to be found. How trite it sounds when I say now that it wasn't out there; it was "in here." The capacity for joy was in my soul even while I was working up a sweat chasing happiness. It was as near as the opportunity to act lovingly, to serve someone else without worrying about whether I was going to be loved, paid, promoted, or elected as a result.

When I remember the awe I felt while being in the same room with the caregivers profiled in *Angels*, I also remember the discovery I made during those years: that it was possible to chase happiness right into hospice. Maybe it was when R. Ellen King sat in her Kansas City office, regaling us with a story about her own cancer, making us all laugh. It was Ellen who inspired this passage in *Angels*:

Some of the funniest hours I've spent, anywhere during my lifetime, have been spent with caregivers. And I mean funny, not just amusing. I'm not talking about slight smiles or quiet chuckles. I'm talking sidesplitting, tummy-grabbing, laugh-until-you-cry, try-not-to-wet-your-pants group guffaws in settings most people avoid because they're afraid of them.

True caregiving is never a job, even when people are paid for it. It is always a special brand of joy.

The joy of serving others begins with getting out of ourselves. I am constantly reminding my self-pity to take a hike. Newspaper columnist Mike Royko claimed once that the motto of Chicago is *Where's mine?* He could have been writing about Wall Street or Main Street—it would apply equally to either. But there's no room for *Where's mine?* when the question you set out to ask is *How can I serve you?*

THE FINAL OF THE Twelve Steps, on which the Betty Ford Center's program is built, is based on one principle: service. Such service, I was taught, comes as a result of "a spiritual awakening," and it enables us "to practice these principles in all our affairs." It establishes the teachings of all twelve-step programs: "The spiritual life is not a theory. We have to live it." In this approach to life, spirituality is service—it is love in action, an experience and not just a feeling. Giving myself to others is evidence that I have actually recovered from the addiction to self-medication, self-centeredness, self-will, and self-pity. It is selflessness.

Late last year I received from a local foundation a lovely tribute for my work in philanthropy. I was humbled, and a little embarrassed because I couldn't attend the award ceremony. Ever gracious, they invited me to give my "acceptance speech" via video. I thought for some time about what to say to these kind friends and neighbors. Most of them knew my story well; I didn't want to reward their kindness with boredom. So instead of another chapter from the Life of Mary, I offered them a story from a different time and place.

A century and a half ago, General William Booth and his wife were suffering through a cold winter in London. Flu was taking lives all around them, famine was following the flu, and funds for General Booth's Salvation Army charity had dried up completely.

Every holiday season General Booth had sent a telegram of encouragement to his colleagues around the world, but this year, he told his wife, "There's not enough money for a single sentence," to which she replied, "Then send a single word."

And so he did.

On a cold December eve, a one-word telegram left London for homeless shelters and feeding stations around the world, sent from Booth to those who did his work in the most desperate of circumstances. It was full of encouragement, because it told the entire mission in a word. And we will thrive, as a community, so long as we remember the lesson Booth knew well.

The word he sent out that night? Others.

When I'm in my studio working, I sometimes feel like a channel between a Divine Force and a final piece of art. It's as if I'm not even in the process, or as if I need to get out of the way. My self needs to be removed. I'm incredibly inspired by these moments. They don't happen on schedule or with much predictability, but they occur often enough to keep me working. They inspire me.

The times I come closest to true service may be when I am planning and then delivering a speech or sermon. I can almost put myself in the text in such a way that I am separated from the self who is there. I stand apart from myself and observe my story, using it to connect to their stories. The experience, especially when I am preaching, is absolutely focused on my listeners. All I care about is them, these others: what they hear, what they experience. It has nothing to do with getting a pat on the back or a standing ovation. This is an absolute desire to serve the person you do not know and likely will never meet, the person who might somehow be touched by a word or changed by a story. If I were to go to the podium or the pulpit looking to hear about splendid results—waiting to hear "You've changed my life!"—I'd already have lost the ideal of service. I'd just be chasing happiness again.

But if I can speak the truth in such a way that others experience with me some of what I experienced in the presence of the *Angels* caregivers, then I will have served. Jennifer Moyer, in some way, will have come back to life. Together we'll have gone to the mountaintop and seen the Promised Land. We will have put love into action one more time, and it will be enough.

15

Doing Something About It

Raised Jewish, I love black preaching. The pitch and cadence of an African-American preacher, voice soaring and whispering, words finding rhythm, moves my soul. That's how I hear James Weldon Johnson's poem "The Creation," where a black preacher remembers a "lonely" God who says, "I'll make me a man." I know a place that is dark and lonesome, before there was light. When the Creator speaks into my darkness, even my dark and lonesome soul becomes creative. Even I can be God's echo.

AS THE AIDS EPIDEMIC quietly reached the age of thirty, my friend Larry Kramer went back to Broadway.

In the spring of 2011, Larry's excruciatingly funny-sad play *The Normal Heart*, staging the first thirty-six months of the epidemic beginning July 1981, reopened with veteran film and TV actress Ellen Barkin making her Broadway debut. The play took home awards galore, including Tonys for Best Featured Revival of a Play, Best Featured Actor (John Benjamin Hickey), and Best Featured Actress (Ellen Barkin).

Many who stumbled from the John Golden Theatre on West Forty-Fifth Street shaken by the final scenes did not recognize the slight, grey-haired man with steely eyes, drawn gaunt by age and surgeries, shoving a piece of paper into every passerby's hand. Larry Kramer, the playwright—and the founder of ACT UP, the AIDS organization once feared by the Establishment—was back on the street in his familiar role of AIDS advocate.

"Thank you for coming to see our play," began the open letter Larry handed theatergoers as they crowded out the center door. "Please know that everything in *The Normal Heart* happened." The drama in the play had not been invented. It came from a faithful depiction: the shocking discovery of "gay cancer," the brutal disinterest of those with power, the humiliation and embarrassments of illness that came before the finality of death. The play showed it all.

It's important to know that Larry had taken his play's title from poet W. H. Auden's "September 1, 1939." Auden had written during the unthinkably dark days when smoke from the ovens of Dachau and Buchenwald drifted lazily over green hillsides where families spread picnic lunches in the warm autumn grass, a time that has led society to question what might be found in the human heart, "the normal heart." Larry lifted Auden's words and passion, wrote a play in 1985, and took to the streets screaming during the days when indifference greeted the dying, the president refused to say the word *AIDS* in public, and hope was a distant stranger. Auden felt the death chill of Hitler, and Larry felt it in his partner's hand while he wasted and died. The point of Larry's play is the final thought of Auden's poem: "There is no such thing as the State and no one exists alone . . . We must love one another or die."

Standing on Forty-Fifth Street in the winter cold, thirty years into the dying, Larry shivered and handed out his letter. "Please know that there is no cure," it read.

Here in America, case numbers continue to rise in every category. In much of the rest of the world . . . the numbers of the infected and the dying are so grotesquely high, they are rarely acknowledged. . . .

Please know that there is no one in charge of this plague. This is a war for which there is no general and for which there has never been a general. How can you win a war with no one in charge?

Please know that most medications for HIV/AIDS are inhumanely expensive and that government funding for the poor to obtain them is dwindling and often unavailable.

Please know that the world has suffered at the very least some 75 million infections and 35 million deaths. When the action of the play you have just seen begins, there were 41. . . .

The screams of ACT UP were the sound of AIDS the year I was diagnosed as HIV-positive. It was so thoroughly viewed as a gay disease in America that the very thought I had contracted the illness was shocking; the reality was beyond thought.

Not so today. By the mid to late 1990s, new HIV infections in the United States were reported to be 8 percent female; today, that figure is about 30 percent female, and the percentage is climbing. AIDS has become an equal-opportunity virus in every sense, including gender equality.

What's particularly tragic about the illness today is that we could stop the dying if we wanted to. The war against AIDS is an utterly winnable war that we are losing. The proof that the war is winnable may be complex, but the primary evidence from the past year or so is simple: In people taking ARVs, the viral load is so suppressed that they are nearly incapable of infecting others. Therefore, what keeps us alive also keeps us from spreading the disease.

When Regan Hofmann, editor of *POZ* ("the AIDS magazine"), wrote an extended piece in the fall of 2011 explaining what would be required "to lay HIV to rest," she had near-universal support. She cited Dr. Anthony Fauci, the National Institutes of Health's AIDS chief, who "said recently in *Science*: 'The fact that treatment of HIV-infected adults is also prevention gives us the wherewithal, even in the absence of an effective vaccine, to begin to control and ultimately end the AIDS pandemic.'"

As Regan concluded, "The critical question is no longer, 'Can we end AIDS?' but 'Will we end AIDS?' Will we garner the political and financial capital to do what science suggests we can?" What stands between us and the end of AIDS, she noted, is "fear of stigma, discrimination, homophobia . . . and death." The fact is, about one million Americans are infected and yet go "untreated with existing drugs that can save their lives and prevent AIDS from spreading," and Regan was absolutely right in calling this "a humanitarian crime of epic proportion."

A million Americans, give or take a hundred thousand, have AIDS and either don't know it or can't get the medicine to treat it. The barriers to treatment have been built over three decades of indifference, stigma, funding cuts, and marginalization of (especially) women and the poor. A million Americans are unnecessarily getting sick, passing on the illness to those they love, and dying. Because AIDS weakens us so other causes can kill us, most obituaries still read *pneumonia* and *cancer*.

It's thirty years into the epidemic and there's a reason Larry Kramer, God bless him, is still on the streets.

I OCCASIONALLY WONDER HOW many years will pass before I no longer hear the phrase *Women can't do that*. It echoes through my life. From earliest childhood my brain was programmed to hear that phrase as a prescription (what women *should not do*) and a fact (what women *aren't capable of doing*).

Born in Kentucky and raised mostly in Michigan during the era of *I Love Lucy* and *Father Knows Best,* I was constantly encouraged to be the type of woman a man wants. *Be cute, be quiet, be good, but don't be too smart or too assertive. Tease, don't compete. Keep your hair stylish and your skirts just long enough.* The "ideal woman" would be, given the lessons I was taught, whatever is "ideal" in the minds of most men, starting with one's father.

Most of those who taught me these lessons were, in fact, women I respected and even loved, including my mother. The men who eventually came into my life—fathers and uncles, then teachers, dates, husbands, bosses—actively and passively affirmed the truth of what I'd been taught by women. To the extent that I could match their ideal, that's what I was: ideal.

My emergence into adulthood coincided with increasingly shrill debates over the Equal Rights Amendment (ERA) prohibiting gender discrimination, eventually passed by Congress (but not ratified by the states) in 1972. By the time I was booking politicians on Detroit's favorite morning TV show, elections were looming and every congressman and senator wanted their views known to women entering the voting booth.

In Michigan, Helen Milliken, the wife of then governor William Milliken, was an outspoken ERA advocate. In Washington, DC, then congressman Gerald Ford's wife, Betty, let it be known to anyone who would listen that the time to pass the ERA was long overdue. Governor Milliken and Congressman Ford, and my father with them, took pride in the fact that the ERA had first been introduced in 1923 by Senator Curtis and Representative Anthony (nephew of Susan B.), both Republicans. Helen Milliken, Betty Ford, and my mother were more inclined to mention that fifty years of male opposition, much of it from Republicans, had prevented ERA approval.

Betty Friedan's surprise best seller a decade previously, *The Feminine Mystique*, is often credited with launching the Women's Liberation Movement. Perhaps. What's certain is that Friedan tapped into the discontent of a generation of women older than I am—my mother's generation. I was fifteen when the book came out (1963), and I didn't read it until much later. Recently, paging through my copy again, I was surprised to see how nonconfrontational it is. Friedan patiently but exhaustively shows that the obligatory "housewife" role assigned to American women—not by their choice, but by social mandate—translated into generations of *Women can't do that*. But this is no manifesto from a female Larry Kramer. She wrote as a woman my mother would have had in for lunch.

I am my mother's daughter, but I am not leading my mother's life. But then, neither is my mother. She was as changed by the rising awareness of women's giftedness as anyone I know. Her life, too, was shaped by the lessons taught to her mostly by women, affirmed mostly by men: that she could climb America's social ladder most quickly in fashionable high heels and a skirt "just long enough." Were she to do it all over again, she would do it differently—not out of unhappiness, but because she could.

During my lifetime not only I, but women, have come to a new understanding of ourselves and our place in the world. Our understanding is not perfect, and it is not finished, but it has happened and continues to happen, and there is evidence of this all around us.

Clearly there are women who hold, for reasons of theology or convenience or culture, that they are inferior creatures when measured against men. And there are men who agree with them. But there are also men and women who spend twelve dollars to become a member and friend of the Flat Earth Society. The evidence is stacked against all of them.

A wise friend once told me that *political change* in places like the U.S. Congress come on the model of a row of dominoes: One senator says, "Yes," and leans on the next senator to agree—and so it goes, one leaning on the next until a majority has fallen. But *social change*, said my friend, comes "like a wind through a forest, knocking down trees in unpredictable patterns. You never see the wind; you just see trees falling." Certainly in the United States, and probably globally, it is this type of *social change* that is lifting women from all stations.

In some settings within Africa and elsewhere, women have held (or been held in) social and economic positions lower than those occupied by cattle. I've met some of these women. Even they are finding ways to discover their equality with men. Stories of husbands hiding cell phones or prohibiting women from using them are rife, but they are also dated: Within a decade, their daughters will be writing computer code in a nearby city. The trees are falling.

When African women look up to see their leaders, women are there. Half of Rwanda's legislature is made up of women because, after the 1994 genocide, the trees were falling. Ellen Johnson Sirleaf came out of prison to become president of Liberia; down goes a tree. A dozen African nations have women as their most senior foreign affairs officer, comparable in position and power to our own secretary of state (who, as I write, is a woman). Everywhere, trees are falling.

I will not ignore the challenges that uniquely face women, from genital mutilation and human trafficking to denial of property rights and rape. Life is not easy for women. But life is not easy. It was not easy in Israel during the formative years when Golda Meir took charge; it was not easy in London when Margaret Thatcher moved in. But compared to a century ago, around the globe, women are rising with greater frequency in more places to higher levels than at any time since monarchies gave way to legislatures.

214

And yet I sometimes fear that we in the United States are slipping backward. As in the AIDS movement, many of the women who called us forward have died or grown silent. In their place I hear commentators charging that those who would elevate the status of women are "liberals." If I call for gender equality, I'm suspected of an assault on everything from motherhood to the papacy.

Despite these cynical voices, I believe that gender equality is broadly accepted in the United States, and that evidence of this acceptance is mostly found not in "women's issues" but in the struggle for equal rights for those who are gay. Most Americans do not know the ERA was never finally approved by the individual states, and most fights over it have ended because women have secured the rights that the ERA would have granted. We won, and we've moved on. The big gender issue in the United States today is gay rights. When I watch states adopt equal marriage options for people who are gay, I am watching social change at work: A tree just fell in New York. Oh, look, a tree toppled over in Vermont. The wind of change is blowing through, and the trees are falling.

I had not expected to live this long. But I'm grateful to be alive, and to have my mother alive with me. Though we came from different generations and lived our different lives, we are women, both of us, who know our equality with men. Our shared task is to mother the changes needed so that all our daughters, everywhere, forever, will be known as the equal of our sons.

I'VE HAD A TWENTY-YEAR-LONG, love-hate relationship with my speech at the Republican National Convention in Houston. August 19, 1992, is a date that has quietly lived within me in both fame and infamy.

The Speech (as it has come to be known in my life) won a measure of approval at the time, and even some momentary fame. In a vast sea of suffering and dying, it was a moment of hope for me—but, really, how good can a single moment be in a sea of suffering and dying?

It seemed in the fall of 1992 that everyone in the world had seen and heard The Speech. Most people thought it was good. But months passed, and then years. Others had their famous moments while I grew older, sicker, and less remembered. By 1996 I couldn't muster a meaningful appearance at the convention in San Diego, and I expected to die before another convention came around. I had accepted the reality of dying, but my acceptance needed to be refreshed with increasing frequency because resentment was growing as my illness progressed.

I resented the idea that my life had peaked in 1992. I resented being defined by a virus. I resented the Republicans for their inaction and the Democrats who blamed me for the Republicans. I resented receiving fewer and fewer invitations to speak and preach. I resented Brian for infecting me, science for not healing me, politicians for ranking me with spoiled fruit. I resented the fact that The Speech eclipsed what may have been better speeches I'd given. I felt as though I'd given "them" (the Republicans, the AIDS community, the advisors, the media) what they wanted, and now they didn't want me anymore. I didn't matter.

Self-pity is easier to drum up when you've not slept for some nights because nausea is fighting with diarrhea, and drugs are dueling with other drugs, and children are being children. However unattractive such self-pity may be, it isn't difficult to find while hugging the porcelain in the bathroom. The Speech did not bring comfort in such moments.

Then came the day I learned the authors of Oxford University's *Words of a Century: The Top 100 American Speeches, 1900–1999* had included The Speech. They had written an incredibly generous introduction describing the event:

> *Within a few minutes, a hush settled over the Astrodome as the delegates stopped chatting and gave Fisher their undivided attention. Some were moved to tears. Across the United States, millions watched on television, captivated by Fisher's poignant words and heartfelt delivery. She reached out to both audiences, speaking at the level of principle rather than partisanship. Her language was elevated, even elegant, her prose lucid and uncluttered, her pacing confident and unhurried. Although some critics caviled that a well-to-do white woman from a privileged family was not representative of most people with AIDS, there can be no gainsaying the artistry or impact of her speech. As the* New York Times *stated, she "took the crusade for decency and compassion into the lion's den. She spoke the message to the people who were most in need of hearing it. For that she has earned our gratitude."*

Grace is love

undeserved.

Grace is the rescue

we **can't perform,**

the comfort

WE CAN'T GRASP.

Their choice brought no money or power. Practically no one knew it had happened; there were no press conferences, no interviews, no congratulatory calls. But being included in that anthology encouraged me to believe that I had used my thirteen minutes in Houston to make a difference.

I think I've come to a place where I can look back at August 19, 1992, with neither exaggeration nor regret, and certainly without self-pity. It's true that I did not change the world, not even the world of AIDS. But I said what needed to be said, to audiences that needed to hear it. I served, which is the source of true satisfaction.

And when I reread The Speech—which I have *very* rarely done—I actually believe it was a moment in which I achieved the goal expressed in these words that hot August night in Texas: "I want my children to know that their mother was not a victim. She was a messenger."

WHAT FINALLY CONQUERS SELF-PITY is gratitude. It's impossible simultaneously to feel grateful and to feel sorry for yourself. I may bridle at the trite slogan *Keep an attitude of gratitude*, but I admit that it is precisely this attitude that most transforms my days and nights into times of serenity.

I look back at The Speech as part of the upside-down experience of life seen in a spiritual light. In a world that defines worth and value by our beauty, our youth, our wealth or power or fame; in a world where we create quarterback heroes and beauty-queen dreams—in this world, the standards have all become upside down.

Perhaps I was "not representative of most people with AIDS," but I was nonetheless the one chosen to speak—by the Republicans and, perhaps, by an even higher Power. As I suggested in a 1996 sermon in Tulsa, Oklahoma, the week of Passover and Palm Sunday:

> *When God comes calling, he calls not for the master but for the slave. When the angel of judgment passes over some and takes others, those who are redeemed are the ones who were despised in the neighborhood, the children abused for the amusement of adults, the women reduced to objects of desire.*
>
> *Over and over, given his choice for a people, God passes over the handsome pharaohs and memorable Cleopatras. He chooses instead to stoop low to pass through a bloody doorway, to lift the broken child and beaten parents, to take the slave by the hand and lead her to the land of milk and honey, feeding her with manna all the way . . .*
>
> *The "good news" that God announces through Passover, and in the week following Palm Sunday, is simply this: God will not leave us alone in our suffering.*
>
> *And this has been my own experience. I would never have asked for AIDS or the suffering. I do not enjoy the memories of my husband's deathbed, or look forward to the day I'll need to leave my children . . .*
>
> *But in the suffering of the AIDS community I have also tasted a grace I never knew. I've found love and courage in others I've met; I was comforted by forgiveness that could rise only from a deathbed. I am, like you, one of those who have met God coming through a bloodied doorpost, near a bloodied cross, where suffering was all that I could see—and now grace is all that I remember.*

The discovery long ago that I was one more weary pilgrim on the road to AIDS could have been very bad news; instead it has turned out to be a pilgrimage toward joy and meaning. This isn't how I would have written my life script, but I was not the Script Writer. Looking back, I see the road to AIDS lined not only with cemeteries but also with moments of grace—even the moment the surgeon explained my cancer.

The healing I've received came, whether from science or spirituality, as a gift, given to me so that I can give to others. That's grace.

I was a woman uncertain of what it meant to be a woman. I was addicted and silent, believing my soul was mute. Then came the gift of art—I did not ask for it, though I welcomed it. And I have embraced my life as a woman and an artist. It's grace, all of it.

The American AIDS community reached out, embraced me, and never let me go. What is that, if not a gift, if not grace? To learn that fear is "just fear," and that depression may be nothing more than a side effect of what was keeping me alive—such lessons are not "earned." Neither is the powerful lesson given in the poetry of W. H. Auden and the theater of Larry Kramer: We must love one another or die. These are lessons we accept with thanks because they are given, not earned. They are grace.

When in a bad moment I am tempted to think nothing matters, including me; when I am ready to give up or give in, and retreat from the world; when I see the children suffering war and the women suffering AIDS, I recall this old Sufi story first told to me somewhere far away:

Past the seeker, as he prayed, came the crippled and the beggar and the beaten. And seeing them, the holy one went down into deep prayer and cried, "Great God, how is it that a loving creator can see such things and yet do nothing about them?"

And out of the long silence, God said: "I did do something about them. I made you."

ABOUT THE AUTHOR

Mary Fisher is known for bringing exuberance, eloquence, and empowerment to the people she encounters, through both her vibrant brand of activism and her extraordinary artistic talent. Her use of inventive techniques and rich juxtapositions of art forms has established her as one of America's most compelling artists, while her compassionate crusade against stigma and shame has placed her firmly among the nation's leading advocates for people affected by the AIDS epidemic. In life as in art, Mary creates work that converts her life experience into a song of the soul.

Born April 6, 1948, in Louisville, Kentucky, and raised in Detroit, Michigan, by her mother, Marjorie, and her father, businessman and philanthropist Max Fisher, Mary attended the Cranbrook Schools, where her earliest experiences as an artist included intensive work with tapestry weaving. As a young woman she attained high-profile jobs as a television producer and an assistant to President Gerald Ford. But by 1980 she had returned to her guiding passion: creating art that imagines and inspires.

Mary was a thriving artist and mother of two young sons when, in 1991, she was diagnosed HIV-positive. Her memorable speech at the 1992 Republican National Convention brought the often hidden struggle with AIDS into millions of living rooms and gave her a new role: ambassador of compassion in the war on AIDS. In the decades since, Mary has carried her message far beyond "the lady who gave that speech," using both artwork and advocacy to raise awareness of the disease and restore dignity to the lives of people, especially women and girls, with HIV/AIDS.

In 1992 Mary founded the Family AIDS Network, a national nonprofit organization dedicated to awakening community, national, and international consciousness to the daily realities facing those who fight the disease. In 2000 the Family AIDS Network was transformed into the Mary Fisher Clinical AIDS Research and Education (CARE) Fund at the University of Alabama at Birmingham, which supports clinical research for people living with HIV and AIDS.

As part of her commitment to enable HIV-positive women to step out of the shadows and empower themselves and their families, Mary has taught the craft of hand-beading jewelry through the ABATAKA Project, which helps women in Rwanda and Zambia acquire job skills and income that allow them to educate, feed, and house their families, and even to start their own small businesses. She showcases the women's handiwork at galleries where her art is exhibited and sells the jewelry on her website as The ABATAKA Collection. Mary also has lent her expertise in textile arts to a project partnering with toymaker Hasbro, Inc., to benefit AIDS orphans in Africa.

Mary has authored five books previously: *Sleep with the Angels* (Moyer Bell, 1994) and *I'll Not Go Quietly* (Scribner, 1995), collections of her speeches and photographs; *My Name is Mary* (Scribner, 1996), an autobiographical memoir; *Angels in Our Midst: A Tribute to Caregivers in Photographs and Stories* (Moyer Bell, 1997); and *ABATAKA* (Copywriters Inc., 2004), stories and artwork inspired by her experiences in Africa. Her powerful speeches have been published in university textbooks and anthologies; her 1992 convention speech is featured in *Words of a Century: The Top 100 American Speeches, 1900–1999* (Oxford University Press, 2008), while her *"Letter to My Sons"* is included in the best-selling collection *Letters of the Century: America 1900–1999* (Dial Press, 2000).

Mary's two sons are now grown: Max, a filmmaker, lives in Michigan, and Zachary, a student, lives in Arizona. Mary and her work have been honored with a variety of awards, tributes, and honorary degrees, including three doctorates. She is a trustee and board member for several national organizations and has served on the Leadership Council of the Global Coalition on Women and AIDS and as an ambassador for the Joint United Nations Programme on HIV/AIDS (UNAIDS).

Mary has spent a lifetime experimenting with new art forms, abstract patterns, and diverse media such as photography, sculpture, prints, beading, handmade paper, and textiles. Her artwork earns frequent mentions in the media, including *More, Quilting Arts, art&culture, Adornment,* and *Town & Country* magazines and The Quilt Show and NowSewing.net webcasts. She has earned special acclaim for her mixed-media approach in both her sculptures and her quilt work, which has been called "astonishing in its message of love, despair, and hope." Her art has been featured in solo and group shows in major galleries around the world, as well as in two presidential museums, in distinguished private and public collections, and in the permanent collection of the UNAIDS headquarters in Geneva, Switzerland. Like any artist looking to continuously evolve her skill, Mary practices her art almost daily at her busy studio in Sedona, Arizona, which has been featured in *Studios* magazine. Her artwork is accessible at www.maryfisher.com.